A General Introduction to the Semeiotic of Charles Sanders Peirce

A General
Introduction
to
the Semeiotic
of
Charles Sanders Peirce

James Jakób Liszka

Indiana University Press
BLOOMINGTON AND INDIANAPOLIS

The paper used in this publication meets the minimum requirements of American National Standard for Information Sciences—Permanence of Paper for Printed Library Materials, ANSI Z39.48-1984.

MANUFACTURED IN THE UNITED STATES OF AMERICA

Library of Congress Cataloging-in-Publication Data

Liszka, James Jakób, date
    A general introduction to the semeiotic of Charles Sanders Peirce.
        p.   cm.
    Includes bibliographical references and index.
    ISBN 0-253-33047-5 (alk. paper)
    1. Peirce, Charles S. (Charles Sanders), 1839–1914—Contributions in semiotics. 2. Semiotics.
P85.P38L57 1996
121'.68—dc20   95-25162

1 2 3 4 5   01 00 99 98 97 96

For my daughter, Alexandra Dylan Liszka

There is a blue in the glacier
That on sun swept days
Colors her eyes
And whose crystalline core
Reflects her person
Just as well as it refracts the light:
Insistent, changing the landscape,
She bends the world to her will.

CONTENTS

PREFACE

However we may want to conceive semeiotic, the goal here is to see it as Charles Sanders Peirce did. Of course this goal cannot be fully realized. Reconstructing the intentions and meanings of the author is not an innocent enterprise. When an author thinks, the products often acquire a life and a sense of their own and make suggestions and connections possibly not anticipated by the author; when the interpreter reads, there is constantly the backdrop of her own horizon. Peirce might be the first to admit this—after all, "thought thinks in us rather than we in it" (CP 5.289n1). But still my idea is to present Peirce's vision of semeiotic as a discipline and to give, as far as possible, a coherent presentation of his theory of signs.

Let's be frank. Peirce's writing is terse and convoluted, without much wit or grace. "I am not naturally a writer," he says, "but as far from being so as any man."[1] "One of the most extreme and lamentable of my incapacities is my incapacity for linguistic expression" (MS 632: 207–209). At times his analyses are so complex and detailed that they seem to make the phenomenon disappear. His examples are obscure and exotic, and so they confuse rather than help. He has a tendency toward digression. As a result I don't quote Peirce as much as I should, although I reference the relevant passages profusely. Where Peirce's own examples are enlightening, I use them; otherwise I devise ones I believe convey the same illustration. Peirce also has an annoying habit of neologizing, which is compounded by the fact that he often gives several names for the same concept. I have tried to include all the alternate usages early on where possible, employing afterward only a single term to represent the idea involved. This makes the initial introduction of terms somewhat cumbersome, but I feel it's important to cross-reference all related terminology.

My goal here is to present Peirce's theory as favorably as possible; the book does not pretend to be a critique of Peirce's general theory. This is not to suggest that it is beyond reproach—certainly there are many flaws and gaps in his account—rather, that the goal is simply to present it sympathetically and in the best light possible. With that accomplished, criticism can be done fairly. I do pay attention to criticisms and scholarly disputes on these matters; however, I have indicated in the endnotes where scholarly controversies exist and have kept the outcome or the best resolution of that controversy in the main text.

I have written the text in the historical present. My choice in doing so is to create a feeling as if Peirce is present and involved in the conversation of the interpretation of his own material. I believe it represents the contemporary influence which Peirce has on modern thinking about signs.

The references to Peirce's work are abbreviated as follows:

CP   *The Collected Papers of Charles S. Peirce.* 8 vols. Vols. 1–6, edited by Charles Hartshorne and Paul Weiss; vols. 7–8, edited by Arthur Burks. Cambridge: Harvard University Press, 1980.

W   *The Writings of Charles S. Peirce.* 5 vols. to date. Vol. 1, edited by Max Fisch et al.; vol. 2, edited by Edward C. Moore et al.; vols. 3–5, edited by Christian Kloesel et al. Bloomington: Indiana University Press, 1980–1993.

LW   *Semiotic and Significs: The Correspondence between Charles S. Peirce and Victoria Lady Welby.* Edited by Charles S. Hardwick. Bloomington: Indiana University Press, 1977.

NEM   *The New Elements of Mathematics.* 4 vols. Edited by Carolyn Eisele. The Hague: Mouton, 1976.

MS   Manuscript numbers correspond to *Annotated Catalogue of the Papers of Charles S. Peirce.* Richard S. Robin. Amherst: University of Massachusetts Press, 1967.

L   References to the correspondence of Peirce.

The best bibliographic source on Peirce's writings on semeiotic and the relevant manuscripts is Fisch, Ketner, and Kloesel (1979). General studies of Peirce's theory of signs, or at least those that involve a preponderance of material on this topic, include Apel (1981), Bense (1967), Fisch (1978), Fisette (1990), Fitzgerald (1966), Greenlee (1973), Savan (1988), and Walther (1974). Full bibliographic details are given in the references section following the endnotes.

I have been a student of Peirce since 1971, when I first encountered him in an undergraduate philosophy class. I immediately recognized an extraordinary mind—but also one of great complexity. This study is the result of a long struggle with Peirce and an ongoing engagement with the community of Peirce scholars, in print and in person. I am especially indebted to David Savan, whose steady and insightful scholarship will be missed and whose encouragement and criticism were so formative; Michael Shapiro, whose teaching and research were a source of regeneration and inspiration; and Nathan Houser, for the cordial discussions of Peirce and helpful guidance through the labyrinth of Peirce's writings. I am grateful to the Peirce Project at Indiana University–Purdue University at Indianapolis, whose facilities and services I have used over the years, in particular to Max Fisch, Christian Kloesel, and Nathan Houser. This book is based in part on a strongly critical reworking of previous studies (Liszka 1978, 1981, 1989, 1990, 1991, 1991a, 1993, 1993a, 1994). I want to thank those colleagues who, over the years, have commented on and criticized this material.

A General
Introduction
to
the Semeiotic
of
Charles Sanders Peirce

1 The Discipline of Semeiotic

Semeiotic as a Formal Science

In one of the more straightforward definitions of semeiotic, Charles Sanders Peirce describes it simply as the formal doctrine of signs (CP 2.227). A *formal* discipline is one that aims at discerning the necessary conditions for the subject it studies (CP 2.227). Since form is "that by virtue of which anything is such as it is" (W 1: 307), formal disciplines are guided by the following question: in order for something to count as whatever it is, what sort of features would it have to have, and, given those features, what are the various ways in which it can be? Semeiotic, so understood, is defined as "the analytic study of the essential conditions to which all signs are subject" (MS 774: 6); its aim is to discern "what *must* be the characters of all signs . . . " and "what *would be* true of signs in all cases . . . " (CP 2.227). Formal sciences are, for this reason, distinct from what Peirce calls the "special" or empirical sciences which do not aim "to find out what *must be* . . . [but] . . . what *is* in the actual world" (CP 2.227). Physics, as an empirical science, may discover what is actually true about motion, but semeiotic (or logic) (CP 2.227), as a formal science, would be concerned, in part, to determine the conditions for counting anything as true.

Peirce considers mathematics the purest and the most exemplary of the formal sciences, since it is "the science which draws necessary conclusions" (CP 4.229) per se, without regard to the factual state of what it studies (CP 4.232). For example, it shows what features are necessary in order for something to count, let's say, as an isosceles triangle, then goes on to show what can be inferred or developed from those features—regardless of whether or not there are, in some sense of the term, isosceles triangles. Mathematics is the study of the form of its own constructions (CP 1.240); it analyzes the form of form. Peirce emphasizes that it is an investigation of hypotheticals (CP 4.232) rather than actualities. "Mathematical form," according to Peirce, "is such a representation of that state of things as represents only the samenesses and diversities involved in that state of things, without definitely qualifying the subjects of the samenesses and diversities" (CP 5.550).

All other formal sciences, including semeiotic (or logic), phenomenology, ethics, aesthetics, and metaphysics, are placed under the rubric of philosophy (CP 1.186, 1.190–192), and are considered derivative formal sciences because they do not study the form of their own constructions but study the form of things already constructed, so to speak. One might label them "reconstructive" formal sciences rather than "constructive" (CP 1.240) ones like mathematics. Phenomenology, for example, aims to show the essential qualities of phenomena abstracted from their particular manifestations, so that no matter how they appear, these features will be present. Semeiotic, similarly, would want to show that no matter how a sign is manifested, for example, as a sound, picture, thought, feeling, action, or naturally occurring event, still the formal conditions which make it a sign would be present.

Each of these disciplines within philosophy shares the same basic character of a formal science, although each is concerned with a different sort of phenomenon: phenomenology "ascertains and studies the kind of elements universally present in . . . phenomenon" (CP 1.186) as such; phenomenology, as "occupied with the formal elements of the phenomenon" (CP 1.284), describes "all the features that are common to whatever is *experienced* or might conceivably be experienced . . . " (CP 5.37). Normative science (including semeiotic, ethics, and aesthetics) "investigates the universal and necessary laws of the relation of phenomena to Ends; that is, to Truth, Right and Beauty" (CP 5.121). More specifically, semeiotic or logic "is the science of the general necessary laws of signs"

(CP 2.39) and is specifically concerned with the relation of phenomena to truth. Metaphysics is concerned to show that "that which is necessarily *true* is part of existential fact, and not merely of thought" (CP 1.489); it sets the necessary conditions for which something which is *logically* possible can be counted as real (cf. CP 1.483).

The Place of Semeiotic in the System of Sciences

In his later years, Peirce was interested in developing a systematic classification of the sciences (see figure 1).[1] His system reflects a very broad, classical sense of "science," not restricted to the modern empirical sciences alone but understood as any attempt to systematize knowledge (CP 1.234). Thus he could include under the label of "science" not only laboratory sciences such as chemistry but also human sciences such as ethnology, as well as disciplines such as history and literary and art criticism (CP 1.201). His schema suggests two main *branches* of science so understood, theoretical and practical (CP 1.239). These are further subdivided into the sciences of discovery, review, and the practical sciences (CP 1.181). The division in terms of branches corresponds to the *purpose* of the science (CP 1.238), so that theoretical sciences aim at the discovery of knowledge, whereas the goal of the sciences of review is the organization of the sciences and the practical ones have as their goal the application of knowledge. The practical sciences are understood by Peirce simply as what we would call applied sciences, such as medicine, engineering, surveying, and navigation (CP 1.243). The sense of "practical" here is clearly more current than the traditional, Aristotelian sense, which included studies such as ethics, politics, rhetoric, and poetics under that rubric. Instead, Peirce treats some of these disciplines as theoretical sciences, for reasons that will become clearer as we proceed. The science of review is a rather odd category. Peirce claims that it is both a theoretical and a practical science (CP 1.202), and not much else is said about it. It is "the business of those who occupy themselves with arranging the results of discovery, beginning with digests, and going on to endeavor to form a philosophy of science. . . . The classification of the sciences belongs to this department" (CP 1.182).

The theoretical sciences are the focus of his work in this regard. Peirce considers a number of sensible frameworks to subdivide the sciences of discovery—for example, in terms of the sort of problem they address (CP 1.227), the kinds of questions they are concerned with (CP 1.184), the technique of reasoning employed (CP 2.644)—but he divides them further

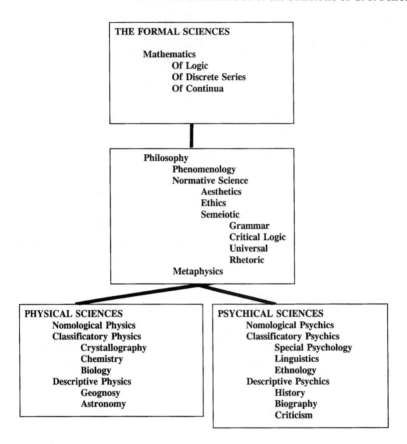

THE FORMAL SCIENCES

Mathematics
   Of Logic
   Of Discrete Series
   Of Continua

Philosophy
   Phenomenology
   Normative Science
      Aesthetics
      Ethics
      Semeiotic
         Grammar
         Critical Logic
         Universal
         Rhetoric
   Metaphysics

PHYSICAL SCIENCES
   Nomological Physics
   Classificatory Physics
      Crystallography
      Chemistry
      Biology
   Descriptive Physics
      Geognosy
      Astronomy

PSYCHICAL SCIENCES
   Nomological Psychics
   Classificatory Psychics
      Special Psychology
      Linguistics
      Ethnology
   Descriptive Psychics
      History
      Biography
      Criticism

Figure 1. Peirce's classification of the theoretical sciences.

into *classes* based primarily on the mode of observation they use (CP 1.239). This strategy is chosen because Peirce believes that "all knowledge whatever comes from observation . . . ," and he agreed with geologist Louis Agassiz that "observation is the 'ways and means' of attaining purpose in science" (CP 1.238). The result is a division of the sciences of discovery into three classes: mathematics, philosophy, and the empirical sciences, according to three different modes of observation.

Mathematics, as we've seen, involves drawing deductive inferences from the observation of its own constructions: " . . . it makes constructions in the imagination according to abstract precepts, and then observes these imaginary objects, finding in them relations of parts not specified in the precept of construction" (CP 1.240). Probably the paradigm which Peirce has in mind here is the geometer who is able to experiment with geometrical diagrams, observe new connections, and make inferences through abstraction and generalization based on those observations (cf. CP 4.233 ff.). He doesn't give a name to this peculiar form of observation, but keeping in line with the other sorts of observational techniques he did name, we might call it *iconoscopic*.[2] As mentioned, mathematics deals with what is logically possible but hypothetically abstract, that is, it seeks only necessary connection between items whose status is merely hypothetical rather than actual.

Mathematics is divided again in terms of *orders*. This sort of division has to do with the particular kind of business or questions the science addresses. Peirce divides mathematics neatly into three concerns: the mathematics of logic (or reasoning), the mathematics of discrete series, and the mathematics of continua.

Philosophy, on the other hand, is concerned to discover not what is hypothetically necessary but actually necessary in regard to the sorts of phenomena it studies, but "it limits itself to so much of truth as can be inferred from common experience" (CP 1.184). For this reason it employs a peculiar kind of observation which Peirce calls *coenoscopic*. This is a kind of observation, typical of the great philosophers, which simply takes the collectivity of common experience and, by processes similar to mathematics, such as abstraction and generalization, is able to draw out its essential qualities, relative to the topic of the observation.

Philosophy also has its *orders*, based on a traditional understanding of its concerns (CP 1.186, 1.280–1.282): philosophy is the formal science of what appears (what Peirce calls *phenomenology*); it is the study of what ought to be (what Peirce calls the *normative sciences*); and it is the formal science of what is, or what is real (Peirce uses the traditional term "metaphysics"). The normative sciences, in turn, have three suborders, corresponding to the classical value trichotomy of truth, goodness, and beauty: logic or semeiotic, ethics, and aesthetics (CP 1.191).

Semeiotic, then, is a suborder of philosophy. It is primarily concerned with the question of truth, which makes it a normative science. That means it is not concerned so much with *what* is true (which is the job of the empirical sciences) but in establishing the conditions for what is to count as true. It is at once an evaluative or normative science (since it establishes criteria for something) and formal, because it attempts to discern the necessary conditions for that norm, a science which aims to establish evaluative norms on the basis of categorical accounts (cf. CP 5.39). In turn, since all thought and knowledge can only take place in signs (CP 1.191, 5.250), then the question of truth really focuses on the formal conditions of signs, their character, their employment, and their transmission and development.

The third *class* of sciences, according to Peirce, comprises what are currently called the empirical sciences, those mostly concerned with what is factually true of the subjects they study, the accumulation of new facts in regard to their particular problems (CP 1.184). This class employs a special kind of observation which Peirce calls *idioscopic* (CP 1.184, 1.242), and so he often calls these sciences by that name. It is the sort of observation that is familiar to any scientist; it requires travel, exploration, or some assistance to the senses, either instrumental or given by training (CP 1.242).

The empirical sciences have two subclasses, the physical and psychical disciplines (CP 1.187, 1.252), a distinction that roughly corresponds to the distinction between the natural and the human sciences.[3] Each subclass is divided in turn by means of the following *orders*: nomological, which is the study of general laws; classificatory, which is the study of general kinds of phenomena, their formation and growth; and descriptive, which endeavors to explain particular, even individual, kinds of phenomena (CP 1.188, 1.189). Among the natural sciences, physics is a good example of a nomological type, since it seeks to discover the ubiquitous phenomena of the physical universe, formulate their laws, and measure their constants (CP 1.188). Chemistry and biology are good examples of classificatory natural sciences, since they attempt to describe and classify certain kinds of physical forms and explain them by laws discovered in physics. Astronomy and geology are descriptive natural sciences, since they aim to study a particular category within the kind which classificatory science studies and, in doing so, applies both the principles of nomological and classificatory sciences to its effort.

This parallels the design among the human sciences (CP 1.257). General psychology is a nomological science, since it seeks to underscore the general laws of the mind (CP 1.199). Linguistics and ethnology are examples of classificatory sciences, since they study kinds of psychological phenomena and are dependent upon the laws of general psychology, according to the understanding of Peirce (cf. CP 1.255). History is an illustration of the last sort of order and so is a descriptive science. The additional subdivisions of history are rather curious (CP 1.201). There is (1) history proper, which includes ancient and modern history, political history, history of the sciences, history of social developments, law, religion, etc.; (2) biography, which, as Peirce suggested, is "at present rather a mass of lies than a science"; and (3) criticism, which he saw as the study of individual works of mind, and included both literary and art criticism.

The Role of Semeiotic in the System of Sciences

" . . . It has never been in my power to study anything—mathematics, metaphysics, gravitation, thermodynamics, optics, chemistry, comparative anatomy, gravitation, astronomy, psychology, phonetics, economics, the history of science, whist, men and women, wine, metrology—except as a study of semeiotic" (LW 85–86). Clearly, then, semeiotic plays a significant role in the system of sciences. What role it plays depends on its position in that system, a system which has a particular hierarchy in mind. As such, two questions must be addressed before we can determine that specific role: *what* is the relation of dependency among the sciences, and *how* are they dependent within that relation?

The relation of dependency among the sciences is defined by the following leading principle, which Peirce borrows from Comte:

> . . . the sciences may be arranged in a series with reference to the abstractness of their objects; and that each science draws regulating principles from those superior to it in abstractness, while drawing data for its inductions from the sciences inferior to it in abstractness. So far as the sciences can be arranged in such a scale, these relationships must hold good. (CP 3.427)[4]

The classification of the sciences is based on three principal divisions: branches, classes, and orders. Consequently, the order within and among each of these divisions should follow this leading principle. Among the branches, the sciences of discovery are superordinate to the other two—and for clear reasons—since they are dependent on the results of the sciences of discovery. Engineering requires the theoretical results of mathematics and physics, just as medicine relies on chemistry, physiology, and biology. Certainly this is clearer in the case of the so-called sciences of review; they are "retrospective" (CP 1.256) and so require an active science to organize.

Among the three classes, mathematics is superordinate, since it "is the most abstract of all the sciences" (CP 3.428). It "meddles with every other science without exception." "There is no science whatever to which is not attached an application of mathematics" (CP 1.245). "Mathematics is the only science which can be said to stand in no need of philosophy . . . " (CP 1.249). Mathematics supplies to the other classes the most abstract and general, formal principles, so that anything which has form (and everything does) would fall, at this level, under its net (cf. CP 3.559). Philosophy, so Peirce reasons, must be superordinate to the empirical sciences, since it deals with principles that are less abstract and general than mathematics

(CP 3.428) but more abstract and general than the laws found in the natural sciences (CP 1.278; cf. 1.514).

In regard to the relation of order to order, the same hierarchical principle is at work as in relations of class to class: the more abstract, the more superordinate. For example, the nomological sciences, such as physics, should be superordinate to the classificatory sciences, such as biology and chemistry, and the latter in turn should be superordinate to the descriptive sciences, such as astronomy and geology. Or, in the case of the human sciences, Peirce argues that linguistics, as a classificatory science, is dependent on general psychology (CP 1.270–271); or, in the case of philosophy, phenomenology, which studies the formal conditions of phenomena as such, should be superordinate to logic or semeiotic, which studies the formal conditions of a particular kind of phenomena, namely signs.

Given the leading principle and the specific suggestions of rank which Peirce makes, we can place semeiotic in relation to the other sciences. In Peirce's schema, semeiotic is dependent on the general principles found in its superordinate class, mathematics (CP 1.186, 1.191), specifically mathematical logic (CP 1.247, 4.228). Within its own class, it is dependent upon the general principles outlined in phenomenology (CP 1.186, 1.191); and within its own suborder, it is dependent upon the normative science of ethics, which in turn is dependent upon aesthetics (CP 1.191). Otherwise all other sciences, either specifically or generally, are dependent upon it. On the other hand, its specific findings will contribute to the refinement of the principles and findings of the sciences superordinate to it.

Depending on whether semeiotic is specifically or generally related to a science its influence will be either direct or indirect; an indirect connection between two sciences could be defined as the case where the one influences a science which directly influences the other. For example, Peirce seems to suggest that the influence of semeiotic is more direct on the human sciences than on the natural sciences (CP 1.250), although certainly the indirect relation is very significant: "It is true that the psychical sciences are not quite so dependent upon metaphysics as are the physical sciences; but, by way of compensation, they must lean more upon logic" (CP 1.250). Metaphysics, as a class within philosophy, is subordinate to logic or semeiotic, but it has more direct connection with the natural than the human sciences. The principal reason for the more direct connection between the human sciences and semeiotic, according to Peirce, is the realization that human and mental phenomena are articulated by purpose and intentionality (what is traditionally called after Aristotle "final causes"), which is the essence of sign activity, while physics is mostly concerned with dyadic, efficient causes. As Peirce puts it succinctly, "The mind works by final causation, and final causation is logical causation" (CP 1.250). Peirce claims that particular human sciences, such as linguistics, are even more specifically dependent on semeiotic (CP 1.250). Consequently, even though everything below semeiotic on the scale of sciences is dependent upon it, the degree of dependency will vary according to the direct or indirect connection of the sciences.

Now *what* is it, in principle, that semeiotic supplies to these other sciences? Again, this depends on the type of connection with a specific science, order, or class of sciences. In its broadest sense, what is true and necessary of signs will be of use to any science which employs signs for its particular purpose; and, of course, every science uses signs as a means of investigation into its particular subject. The physicist employs signs in her observations, instrumentation, inferences, conclusions; in terms of the expression and communication of each of these; in terms of the justification and establishment of its findings. This is true of any science qua science. Semeiotic can offer a guide and a framework for each of these general concerns. But also it can offer more specific help to particular disciplines whose business is to study certain sorts of signs. This is especially true of the human sciences. With this understanding, it could be said that physics studies natural signs, psychology mental signs, linguistics verbal signs, anthropology socially conventional signs, art criticism visually aesthetic signs. The point is that the findings of semeiotic at the formal level would have specific application to the study of specific kinds of signs; and, conversely, the findings of these specific sciences would add to the refinement and adjustment of formal semeiotic. But, in a general sense, the results of semeiotic are applicable to any science, and it is for this reason "the coenoscopic science of sciences" (CP 8. 343).

The Divisions of Semeiotic

Semeiotic is a normative science which is an order within the class of philosophic sciences. As a normative science it is concerned with the first of the primary values—truth, goodness, beauty. But, according to Peirce, it is concerned with truth in three regards, which define three branches of the discipline (CP 1.191): the study of the sign's grammar, logic, and rhetoric. This parallels the classical trivium in liberal studies,[5] although of course with reference to the sign. Grammar is the study of the formal features of the sign and its modes of expression; logic is concerned with the manner in which signs can be used to discern truth; while rhetoric is the investigation into the manner in which signs are used to communicate and express claims within a community. These studies are variously named by Peirce, but the preferred usages here will be *semeiotic grammar*, *critical logic*, and *universal rhetoric*. These divisions are probably more familiar to many readers under Charles Morris's nomenclature: syntax or syntactics, semantics, and pragmatics.[6]

Peirce has several names for the first division. This is called variously by Peirce *speculative grammar* (CP 1.191, 1.559, 2.83, 2.206, 2.229, 2.332), *pure grammar* (CP 2.229), *formal grammar* (CP 1.116, 8.342, 1.559), *universal grammar* (W 1: 175, 1: 274), *general grammar* (W 1: 304), and *stechiology* (NEM 4: 20–21). The concern of semeiotic grammar is to determine the formal conditions for signs as such: "the general conditions of signs being signs" (CP 1.444); "those conditions without the fulfillment of which [signs] would not be signs at all" (MS 1147A: 111). As the name suggests, it would function much in the way in which the grammar of a language establishes the rules for meaningful speech. Put differently, its goal is to ascertain what must be true of signs in order for them to embody meaning (CP 2.229), to determine "the formal conditions of symbols having meaning" (CP 4.116). This includes the study of the basic components of signs, their types, aspects, and classification.

The second division of semeiotic is logic proper (CP 2.229), variously called *critic* (CP 1.191, 2.92) or *general logic* (W 1: 304). This is concerned with the necessary conditions by which signs can tell us something truthful about the objects they represent (CP 2.229); it attempts to discern those conditions "without the fulfillment of which [signs] would not be signs of the object intended (that is, would not be true)" (MS 1147A: 111). Not only do we think only in signs, but *how* we think in signs is the concern of this aspect of semeiotic: "begin, if you will, by calling logic the theory of the conditions which determine reasoning to be secure" (CP 2.1). As such it involves the analysis of the various sorts of reasoning processes, the classification of arguments and their evaluation (CP 1.191, 2.203). This is certainly the most normative aspect of semeiotic because it aims to establish criteria for good thinking (that is, thinking which, for the most part, arrives at the truth) versus bad thinking (that which for the most part leads to error). One might say, generously speaking, that critical logic, or logic proper, is the attempt to decipher the means by which we may avoid error, eliminate illusion and distortion, and positively ascertain the truth.

The third division of semeiotic is variously called *speculative rhetoric* (CP 2.93, 2.105, 2.333, 2.356), *methodeutic* (CP 2.93, 2.105, 2.207, 1.191), *formal rhetoric* (CP 1.559, 1.116, 8.342), *general rhetoric* (W 1: 304), *universal rhetoric* (W 1: 274), and *objective logic* (CP 1.444). Peirce argued that it should be understood generally as the study of "the necessary conditions of the transmissions of meaning by signs from mind to mind" (CP 1.444); or, as the study of "the formal conditions of the force of symbols, or of their power of appealing to mind . . . " (CP 1.559); or, its task is "to ascertain the laws by which . . . one sign gives birth to another, and especially one thought brings forth another" (CP 2.229). So, whereas semeiotic grammar is the study of what must be true for signs qua signs and critical logic is the study of the conditions for the proper use of signs, or truth, formal rhetoric is the study of the formal conditions under which signs can be communicated, developed, understood, and accepted.

Semeiotic as a Coenoscopic Science

There is certainly a question of how semeiotic arrives at its results and how these results might be justified. For example, what are the processes involved in arriving at a certain classification of signs, and what sort of guarantee do we have that it is a fairly accurate account? This is an especially difficult issue in semeiotic, since it is a sort of bootstrap science; it must formulate the general principles which are necessary for concluding anything about or from signs by means of principles and reasonings which are the subject of its own investigation. Even though it does get some direct guidance from phenomenology, especially the so-called doctrine of categories, and indirect guidance from mathematics (that is, not necessarily the results but the methods and procedures in mathematics), still it is left with this basic paradox: that it must justify its own findings by means of the principles which it attempts to discover and analyze.

But as a science it must, like any other science, engage in three basic processes: making observations, reasoning on the basis of those observations, and providing confirmation of the results of that reasoning, that is, determining which results of the reasoning are true (cf. CP 7.327–335). These processes, observation, inference, and justification, we assume, are universal to any sort of investigative science (although they are fairly well defined in the case of the laboratory and experimental natural sciences), that is, to all three classes of science.

Consider first the process of observation in regard to semeiotic. As a subclass of philosophy, semeiotic shares with the other members of the class the same basic method of coenoscopic observation. This, as mentioned, involves the ability to analyze a particular phenomena on the basis of the collectivity of ordinary experience and the accumulation of traditional understanding. This, as Peirce noted, makes philosophy and semeiotic "eminently fallible" (CP 2.227). Like it or not, this seems to summarize the method of observation employed by most philosophers, from Plato and Aristotle to Foucault and Derrida. For example, when Aristotle attempts to define a symbol in *On Interpretation*, it is clear that it is an analysis using abstraction and generalization and is based on a common experience of how language works, with an eye toward those who have attempted it before him. The same could be said of Derrida's similar attempt in *On Grammatology*. This peculiar ability—which the great philosophers share— to abstract and generalize is a reflection of the sort of skill found in mathematics (CP 2.227). To put it simply, we could say that observation is the name for the collection of different types of operations involved in the *analysis* of a phenomenon, and *coenoscopic* observation involves the analysis of common human experience in regard to a certain kind of phenomenon. Certainly these same types of operations involved in the analysis of phenomena are present in the process of observation as found in the empirical sciences, although they employ the aid of instrumentation and involve a more restricted and delimited phenomena; they are also present in mathematics (CP 4.235 ff.), although in a purer form and, again, the phenomena are imaginatively created rather than found in nature or culture. That these operations are themselves the subject of analysis by (critical) logic or semeiotic makes it a bootstrap process.

Some of these analytic operations are familiar enough; others have names rather original to Peirce (most of them will be discussed in chapter 3). Primary among these operations is *abstraction*, which has two species, according to Peirce: *prescisive abstraction* and *hypostatic abstraction* (CP 4.235). The first involves the process by which we think of a particular nature (e.g., sweetness) without regard to its individual manifestations (CP 2.428); the second involves the attribution of the prescinded property to a particular kind of phenomena with which it was originally associated in the observation (e.g., honey possesses sweetness) (CP 4.235). Generalization, or *ascent*—not to be confused with induction (CP 2.429)—is the process by which we extend the reference of the prescinded property while attenuating its sense or meaning (e.g., sugar also possesses sweetness, although not exactly the same sort of sweetness as honey). *Descent*, on the other hand, is the process by which we develop the peculiar sense of sweetness in the context of a particular kind of phenomena (e.g., honey possesses a soft, musty sweetness), that is, we increase the sense while restricting its reference (CP 2.429). Peirce provided a list of several other operations in this regard (a matter detailed a bit later), but this sample, perhaps, provides a general sense of the idea involved.

In regard to the second aspect of any science, inference, Peirce devoted a great deal of thought to this matter. Observations typically produce singular propositions of the form S is P (e.g., honey is sweet),[7] while inference involves a conclusion (of the form S is P) drawn from other propositions (since honey is sweet, and sweet things ought to be tasted, honey should be tasted) (cf. CP 2.420, 2.423, 7.331, 7.333). Investigation involves, besides observation, "the production of new beliefs out of old ones according to logical laws. This process is the *logical process*, but by an extension of the meaning of a familiar word I call it also *inference*" (CP 7.331n9). In general, observation introduces new ideas or "facts," while inference combines these with others in order to draw out new propositions. Inference has three basic forms: abduction, deduction, and induction (cf. CP 2.266, 2.774). *Abduction* is the process of reasoning that is involved in the formulation of a hypothesis or general proposition that seeks to account for a surprising or anomalous observation. It attempts to resolve the anomaly or puzzle by means of a preliminary conclusion: "[abduction] is where we find some very curious circumstance, which would be explained by the supposition that it was a case of a certain general rule, and thereupon adopt that supposition" (CP 2.624). By *induction*, "we conclude that facts, similar to observed facts, are true in cases not examined" (CP 2.636). *Deduction* is a form of reasoning such that "the facts presented in the premises could not under any imaginable circumstances be true without involving the truth of the conclusion" (CP 2.778).

These three types of reasoning are present in all the sciences, but depending on the type of class they will be manifested differently. For example, these are certainly present in mathematics—which serves as a good example, since semeiotic, as a formal science, has more in common with it than with the empirical sciences. The process (in pure mathematics) is as follows (CP 2.778): we form in the imagination some sort of diagrammatic representation of the facts, as abstract as possible; the diagram is then observed, and a hypothesis suggests itself that there is a certain relation between some of its parts. In order to test this, various experiments are made upon the diagram, which is changed in various ways. The last procedure, as Peirce noted, is "extremely similar to induction, from which, however, it differs widely, in that it does not deal with a course of experience, but with whether or not a certain state of things can be imagined" (CP 2.778). Again, this is due to the difference in *class* of science; similarly, we would expect the same sorts of procedures in the investigation of signs, except that, instead of the imaginary, schematic phenomena of mathematics or the delimited phenomena of the natural sciences, the phenomena involved are those of our everyday common experience of signs.

Finally, there is the question of justification, the matter of establishing the truth of a claim in a particular science. Just as the other two aspects of investigation are considered by Peirce to be common to any science (although modified depending on the class of science), so it is with issues of justification. For semeiotic (specifically critical logic, but also universal rhetoric), this will involve the broader issues of justification, the justification of a certain method of inquiry (cf. CP 7.326), a justification of each of the kinds of inferences or arguments (abduction, deduction, and induction), that is, their *validity* (CP 2.780), as well as establishing criteria for evaluating the results of particular arguments, their *strength* (CP 2.780). Finally, it would also seek to establish criteria for evaluating the *truth* of particular *propositions* (as opposed to the validity of arguments which might employ true propositions). Again, in this regard semeiotic must act like a bootstrap science: if one of the goals of semeiotic is a normative evaluation of these methods and means for establishing the truth of propositions, then, it would have to apply the criteria it establishes to its own investigations. Semeiotic is *the* pivotal discipline in this regard, since its results establish criteria for inquiry, argument, and truth, essential for any investigation, yet its results must undergo the scrutiny of its own findings.

A General Characterization of Semeiotic

Perhaps it will now be easier to summarize the general character of semeiotic. Semeiotic, as a branch of philosophy, is a formal, normative science that is specifically concerned with the question of truth as it can be expressed and known through the medium of signs, and serves to establish leading principles for any other science which is concerned with signs in some capacity.

As a formal science it is interested in determining those necessary and essential conditions of the character and employment of signs. It has three branches in this regard, the study of the necessary conditions which count anything as a sign as such (semeiotic grammar), the establishment of criteria for counting something as true by inferences from and through signs (critical logic), and the determination of the conditions for the communication and development of signs (universal rhetoric).

Semeiotic is primarily a normative science, since it is concerned with signs in regard to the question of truth value. This means that it deals not only with the description and characterization of signs (as in semeiotic grammar) but also with their proper employment in inquiry and the means by which they should be used to persuade and achieve consensus.

As a subclass of philosophy, semeiotic is a coenoscopic science, meaning that it draws upon common everyday experience of signs as its data base, so to speak, and, employing operations such as abstraction, generalization, and the general kinds of inferences common to any inquiry, seeks to establish its (fallible) findings about the character of signs and the criteria for their employment.

Semeiotic is a pivotal science, since its role in the system of sciences is to provide leading principles for any investigation that studies particular kinds of signs or draws upon signs for *its* principles. At the same time it uses the results of the subordinate sciences to refine its own findings. Semeiotic receives its leading principles from mathematics and phenomenology and its normative guides from ethics and aesthetics. In turn, the results of the study of signs supply these superordinate sciences with materials that will help refine their findings.

Semeiotic and Semiology Compared as a Discipline

It is imperative to compare Peirce's sense of semeiotic as a science with Ferdinand de Saussure's ideas concerning *semiology* as a discipline,[8] since Saussure is considered to be an independent founder of the study of signs and his great influence on other thinkers is manifest.[9] Saussure's classic definition of semiology is "a science that studies the life of signs within society." Consequently, semiology is a part of social psychology, which is a branch of general psychology. As Saussure insisted, "to determine the exact place of semiology is the task of psychology." On the other hand, linguistics is only a part of the general science of semiology, and the task of the linguist is to find out what makes language a special system with the mass of semiological data (1959: 16).

Semiology is concerned with the study of signs, but for Saussure, signs are primarily a psychological entity (1959: 8), since they are the association or correlation between an *idea* and some sign. In this sense semeiotics is subordinate to a general and perhaps even an individual psychology. But, on the other hand, to the extent that a system of such associations between idea and sign is *conventional*, the latter being a collective product (1959: 14), then semiology is dependent upon social psychology. Linguistics is the study of a certain kind of conventional correlation, that between idea and sound; consequently it is subordinate to semiology. Semiology is, then, concerned with a certain kind of convention that is responsible for the production of signs within human society.

As noted, Peirce sees semeiotic as supplying leading principles to sciences such as general and social psychology and linguistics; it also serves to establish criteria by which such investigations can derive good results from the employment of signs and shows, in general, the formal character of signs as such. So one might say that for Peirce the relation between linguistics and semeiotic is one of discipline to methodology, or empirical science to formal science, whereas for Saussure the relation is one of general to particular discipline. Peirce certainly believes this to be true of the relation between psychology and linguistics (CP 1.189), but not between semeiotic and linguistics. In Saussure's framework, semiology would yield general empirical laws which could then be applied to the specifics of linguistics. Thus semiology, too, would be a special, empirical science, somewhat on the order of psychology. For Peirce, semeiotic is an organon (to use Aristotelian nomenclature), which can then be applied across disciplines. Presumably for Saussure, semiology is not applicable to the physical sciences, and it is subordinate to psychology. For Peirce, semeiotic is applicable to the physical sciences as well (although it is more directly applicable to the psychical sciences) and, indeed, by allowing a much wider concept of sign to include, besides conventional signs, natural and nonhuman ones as well, Peirce envisioned semeiotic as a more comprehensive study whose results would be employed by the several empirical disciplines.

This is clearly contrary to claims made by some that the two disciplines are synonymous.[10] Pierre Guiraud declares that "Saussure emphasized the social function of the sign, Peirce its logical function. But the two aspects are closely correlated and today the words semiology and semiotic refer to the same discipline" (1975: 2). This seems to imply that the dispute between the two accounts is merely one of nomenclature. The question, then, is whether these two distinct accounts of the discipline are incompatible (cf. Martinet 1980) or compatible, and if so, whether they are complementary (Culler 1981: 24, Merrell 1990: 96) or hierarchically dependent.

The only way in which the logical or formal view of semeiotic and the empirical one would be compatible is if the empirical and the formal were treated as the same. This is generally called the theory of psychologism; it is something Peirce argues fervently against (see CP 2.39–54), and it is something with which Saussure had no concern. Actually, psychologism has grown to have three senses. The first, original sense was developed in the early nineteenth century by Jakob Fries (1824) and Friedrich Beneke (1833), who argued that philosophy, generally speaking, should be treated as a branch of psychology, since philosophy primarily uses mental reflection, introspection, and self-observation, which are psychological processes. The second sense, which is the dominant sense of the term, was articulated by John Stuart Mill and others in the late nineteenth century; it argues that psychological processes are the only basis for formulating and justifying the basic principles of logic.[11] A third sense is more a question of territorial dispute, suggesting that anything produced by the mind falls within the domain of psychology proper.

Certainly Saussure could be accused of the third sense of psychologism, which is the kind of psychologism Leonard Bloomfield accused him of in regard to the relation of linguistics and psychology (1935: 19). But Peirce could be accused of this same sort of psychologism, since he classifies linguistics in the same way. On the other hand, Peirce argues strongly against Mill's version of psychologism, but Saussure had no interest in this issue. Peirce gives what we would now consider standard arguments against Mill's psychologism. First, logic in the main has to do with how we *ought* to think, while psychology studies how we *do* think. Psychology is an empirical science, logic mostly a normative science (CP 2.51). Second, using a distinction also found in Frege (and Herbart), Peirce argued that logic had nothing to do with thinking processes but was concerned with the formal relations among thoughts, independently of how they were thought or produced (CP 2.53). By treating a sign in its formal characteristics, we do not pay attention to its particular mode of production, and thus a formal analysis has wider (although more general) application to particular instances. To take a very simple example, we can say that an icon is a relation between a sign and its object based on some rule of similarity; but actual icons can be produced in a number of different ways: mentally, phonetically, graphically, pictorially, etc. In general, the formal, logical view allows that a sign need not be just a mental phenomenon or a social phenomenon or a biological phenomenon, expressible as such. This formal view of the sign entertains a wider understanding of the sign and sign processes as having a relatively objective set of rules and structures which are then manifested or realized in the data of a number of empirical disciplines, ranging from astronomy to zoology.

Also, by implication, Peirce would argue against the Beneke and Fries sense of psychologism. Although it is true that philosophy as a coenoscopic science uses reflection, introspection, and self-observation, these processes of observation are nonetheless inferential and therefore subject to normative (and so semeiotic) evaluation. More specifically, processes such as abstraction, prescision, ascent, descent, and extension can be categorized, analyzed, and evaluated like any other reasoning process.

2 Semeiotic Grammar

The General Formal Conditions of Signs

Semeiotic grammar is concerned with determining the formal conditions for signs as such (CP 1.444). In order for a *sign* or *representamen*[1] to count as a sign it must have four formal conditions, according to Peirce. At least three of these are based on early work on his doctrine of categories: "everything has some character," "everything stands in relation to something," and "everything may be comprehended or more strictly translated by something" (W 1: 332–333). The four conditions are: (1) A sign must correlate with or represent an object (CP 2.230; W 1: 287). This might be called the *representative* condition of the sign. This argues that all signs have a directedness toward objects, or at least purport to be about something.[2] (2) The sign must represent or correlate with that object in some respect or capacity (its *ground*) (CP 2.228, 3.361). Every sign must have some sense or depth in order to count as such (W 1: 287). This might be called its *presentative* condition. (3) The sign must determine (potentially [CP 2.92] or actually) an *interpretant* (CP 2.228, 2.308, 5.253), understood as a sign which translates and develops the original sign. A sign must have the ability to create another equivalent or more developed sign, in some interpreter (CP 2.228), which articulates the original sense and reference, breadth and depth. In order to be a sign it must represent something to some sign user, i.e., something which represents the representation as a representation (W 1: 323). This might be called its *interpretative* condition. (4) The relation among sign (in regard to its ground), object, and interpretant must be *triadic*, that is, thought of as an irreducible interrelation through which each component gets its sense (CP 5.484), so that the sign's power to represent is mediated by its grounding and interpretation and, similarly, for each of the other components.[3] Each of the first three formal conditions of the sign is mediated through the others: the ability of the sign to represent also requires, inherently, its power to be *interpreted* as a sign of that object *in some respect*; the ability of the sign to be interpreted can only work if it is interpreted as *representing* an object *in some respect*; and it can only be understood as representing an object in some respect if it is *interpreted* as *representing* an object as such. Thus grounding, representation, and interpretation are triadically interdependent. So, in its most general and fullest terms, a sign must represent something in some respect to some interpreter in order to count as a sign (CP 2.228). This might be called its *triadic condition.*

Most of Peirce's formal definitions of sign include these four essential components:[4]

> A *sign* . . . is a First which stands in such a genuine triadic relation to a Second, called its *Object*, as to be capable of determining a Third, called its *Interpretant*, to assume the same triadic relation to its Object in which it stands itself to the same Object. The triadic relation is *genuine*, that is its three members are bound together by it in a way that does not consist in any complexus of dyadic relations. (CP 2.274)
>
> [a sign is] anything which is related to a Second thing, its *Object*, in respect to a Quality in such a way as to bring a Third thing, its *Interpretant*, into relation to the same object. . . . (CP 2.92)
>
> A sign therefore is an object which is in relation to its object on the one hand and to an interpretant on the other in such a way as to bring the interpretant into a relation to the object corresponding to its own relation to the object. (LW: 32)

Something becomes a sign not because of any inherent feature it has but because it acquires the formal characteristics that any sign must have, namely, that it correlate with an object and that it produce an interpretant in a process in which the three are irreducibly connected. Only when it acquires these formal characteristics, then its conventional, inherent, or natural characteristics may contribute to making it a certain kind of sign. But for this reason signs are not natural kinds in the way in which a star or an elephant is. Both stars and elephants may become signs in addition to being whatever they are apart from that. Thus anything can become a sign, and most everything does (and so Peirce's well-known claim that the universe is "perfused with signs"): "sign[s] . . . includes pictures, symptoms, words, sentences, books, libraries, signals, orders of command, microscopes, legislative representatives, musical concertos, performances of these" (MS 634: 18). So semeiotic grammar, as Peirce claims, "studies the ways in which an object can be a sign" (MS 774: 6) and the way in which it can become a sign is if it expresses these formal characteristics.

The Ground of a Sign
(the Presentative Condition)

The sign always presents its object *as* that object in some regard or respect, and so serves to present its object aspectively and partially. For example, the sign (in this case a proposition) "This stove is black" presents the stove in terms of a certain quality, blackness, that is imputed to it by the sign (cf. CP 1.551). By presenting the object *as* black, the sign selects certain features, characters, or qualities of the object.[5]

However, it presents these qualities or characteristics of the object *in the sign* in an abstract form. The ground[6] of the sign is an abstract quality or form of the sign (CP 1.551, W 1: 522), somewhat in a quasi-Platonic sense of form (CP 2.228). Peirce puts it in a more precise way: the ground when prescinded from its object is a pure form or idea (W 1: 335). Or, as he says it somewhat metaphysically,

> character is the ground of being; whatever is, is by being *somehow*. . . . Character is then always a ground, and as ground is also always a character; the two terms are coextensive. Reference to a ground, i.e., possession of a character is not a conception given in the impressions of sense but is the result of generalization. (W 1: 352–3, 1: 479, 1: 521–522)

The ground, as the presentation of the object, thus serves as the *basis* upon which the sign can represent its object,[7] or as Peirce writes, "ground" is the "reason which determines [the sign] to represent that object to that subject" (W 1: 327). "The immediate function of reference to a ground is to unite relate and correlate, and hence its introduction is justified by the fact that without it reference to a correlate is unintelligible" (W 1: 353); "no relation can have place without a quality or reference to a *ground* " (W 1: 522). The presentation of the object in the sign serves then as the basis for its representation. By "characterizing" the object, the sign allows itself the possibility of being connected to it and, at the same time, reveals a certain sense or connotation in regard to that object (W 1: 479, CP 2.418).

The Object of a Sign
(the Representative Condition)

The second essential formal feature of a sign is that it must correlate or represent an object. Peirce has a very wide understanding of what an object can be: it may be a

> single known existing thing or thing believed formerly to have ex-
> isted or expected to exist, or a collection of such things, or a known
> quality or relation or fact, which single object may be a collection,
> or a whole of parts, or it may have some other mode of being, such
> as an act permitted whose being does not prevent its negation from
> being equally permitted, or something of a general nature desired,
> required, or invariably found under certain general circumstances.
> (CP 2.232)

In other words, an object of a sign can be nearly anything, and what makes something an object *of a sign* is the fact that it is *represented* as such by the sign (the result being the so-called *immediate object* of the sign) and that it serves to offer resistance, to provide a constraint, or, in general, to act as a determinant for the process of semeiosis which represents it, in which case it is called the *dynamic object* (CP 8.314, 8.343, 4.536). The immediate object is the object viewed from the context of the sign—its representative content—while the dynamic object can be considered as the dynamism, the machine that drives the semeiotic process; it is what compels the sign (CP 5.554). The dynamic object of the sign is the invisible hand which, in the long run, guides the semeiotic process to a final determination concerning any information or signification concerning that object—even if that means the interpretation of the sign fails to generate any positive information. But just because it is a dynamism does not mean that it has to be understood always as an individual thing that has the capability of exerting physical force. It can be a dynamism of different phenomenological types (LW 83–84): it is feasible that a possible can act as a dynamic object, just as it is likely than an actual existent can act so or a general law. For example, a goal not yet achieved might be considered a possible which nonetheless serves to determine representations of it. Hamlet, for example, in the sense of the collection of words and deeds which a certain character performs in a Shakespeare play, can act as a dynamic object, even though Hamlet is fictional (which in a sense is a possible). There is a tendency to treat the dynamic object as if it were a "real" object—and Peirce is not entirely consistent on this matter[8]—but, overall, he wants to sort out the difference between something being real and something being a dynamic object.[9]

The division of objects allows us to view the sign from two aspects: the object from the perspective of its *representation* in the sign, and the object as the *determinant* of the sign, the so-called process of *determination* (understood as a process of constraint rather than causation) (cf. MS 499). There is a variety of senses of "representation" in Peirce (W 1: 174; CP 1.553, 2.230, 2.273, 2.295). Sometimes Peirce uses the word as a synonym for sign (cf. W 1: 174); sometimes he speaks as if representation is nothing more than the substitutability of sign for object (cf. CP 2.273). He also seems to make a distinction between denotation and representation (cf. CP 2.295).[10] It is probably safer to characterize representation as the sign's "connectedness" to an object, its relatedness, its intentionality, or its purported "aboutness" (cf. W 1: 286–287). The connectedness is estab- lished not only by physical or causal means but also by similarity or convention. This connectedness allows the possibility of reference, al- though not all signs will successfully refer (W 1: 287). Determination, on the other hand, is a forward-looking process of constraint placed initially by the dynamic object upon some sign, which then carries within it, so to speak, the seed of further determination: "a sign is something which brings a determination of one thing into correspondence with another thing which determined [it]" (MS 286V 545). The dynamic object is that which *compels* the sign, the way in which an order compels the subordinate to obey it (CP 5.554).

Representation is possible only through the mediation of grounding and interpretation. The sign can only be said to represent its object if there is an interpretant which correlates the two. But that can be done only if there is ground upon which to make that correlation. The grounding in turn requires an object having the characteristics which make the ground- ing possible. This can be thought of a bit differently. The grounding by the sign *determines* the interpretant in such a way that such a correlation can be established; on the other hand, the object determines the sign in such a way that its grounding is possible (cf. MS 318: 81). Consequently the effect of representation is created when these two processes are co-present. The sign's ability to represent, then, is established mediately, through the sign's ability to determine an interpretant which can interpret the sign as correlative with the object.

Determination should be understood as a constraining rather than a causally deterministic process, as the term might suggest (cf. CP 8.177). Sometimes Peirce speaks as if determination is a simple linear process in which the dynamic object determines the immediate object, which in turn determines the sign, which then determines the interpretant (LW: 84). But a more complex analysis is given in the following passage: the sign "is *determined* by the object relatively to the interpretant, and *determines* the interpretant in reference to the object, in such a way as to cause the interpretant to be determined by the object through the mediation of the sign" (MS 318: 81). This suggests a more complicated mediation of the elements of semeiosis in the determinative process. In its relation to the object, the sign is passive, "that is to say, its correspondence to the Object is brought about by an effect upon the sign, the Object remaining unaffected. On the other hand, in its relation to the interpretant, the sign is *active*, determining the interpretant without being itself thereby affected" (MS 793: 2–3).

Determination of the sign should be distinguished from sign *production*. The production of a sign is the causal result of the interaction between a dynamic object and the sign medium of some sign-interpreting agency. The dynamic object, *ceteris paribus*, will offer the same modus of constraint despite different signs produced by the interaction with the medium. The bee's perception of a flower will differ from a human's (due to difference in the range of wavelength perception), but the constraint offered by the dynamic object for each will be the same. Put succinctly, the difference in wavelength of light emanating from one part of the flower to another determines the contrast seen in the immediate object of the sign, although the contrast in the bee's sign and the human's sign will differ markedly. To take another simple example, if the level of gasoline in a gas tank is considered the dynamic object, then various signs produced by it will reflect the same constraint; supposing that the tank is half full, tapping the tank will produce a difference in sound pitch that corresponds to that level; or a gauge, due to the difference in the pressure from the level of liquid, will push its needle to the halfway point. In both cases, the dynamic object (the level of liquid in the tank) offers the same constraint to the sign, despite the different media. The sign in turn imparts a certain determination to the interpretant. Any interpretant of the sign is guided by the determination which the dynamic object imparts to the sign: the difference in sound pitch will correlate to the differences in volume of gasoline; the position of the needle on the gauge will correspond to the differences in volume of the gasoline, etc. In other words, determination guides the representation of the object. Determination provides the form (what I believe Peirce means as the basis of the ground), the hook, so to speak, upon which the sign can hang its representation of the dynamic object:

> That which is communicated from the Object through the Sign to the Interpretant is a Form; that is to say, it is nothing like an existent, but is a power, is the fact that something would happen under certain conditions. This Form is really embodied in the object, meaning that the conditional relation which constitutes the form is true of the form as it is in the object. In the sign it is embodied only in a representative sense, meaning that whether by virtue of some real modification of the Sign, or otherwise, the Sign becomes endowed with the power of communicating to an interpretant. (MS 793: 2–4)

Peirce sometimes speaks loosely and metaphorically as if something "emanates" from the object into the sign in this sense: "in every case an influence upon the Sign emanates from its Object, and . . . this emanating influence then proceeds from the sign . . . and produces an effect that may be called the Interpretant, or interpreting act, which consummates the agency of the Sign" (MS 634: 23, cf. CP 2.230). A different way of articulating this is by saying that the dynamic object as a determinant grounds the sign, and this grounding provides the fabric for representation. As the fourth formal principle (the triadic principle) suggests, the sign can only be said to represent its object if there is an interpretant which correlates the two, and that can be done only if there is ground upon which to make that correlation. This grounding is the *effect* of the dynamic object, the determination by the dynamic object.

The Interpretant of the Sign (the Interpretative Condition)

Every sign in order to be a sign must be interpreted as such (CP 2.308). In other words, every sign must be capable of determining an interpretant. The interpretant can be understood in its most generous sense as the *translation* of a sign: "a sign is not a sign unless it translates itself into another sign in which it is more fully developed" (CP 5.594); "meaning . . . [is] in its primary acceptation the translation of a sign into another system of signs" (CP 4.127); "the meaning of a sign is the sign it has to be translated into" (CP 4.132); "there is no exception to . . . the law that every thought-sign is translated or interpreted into a subsequent one . . . " (CP 5.284). Translation can be understood in three different ways. The interpretant is determined by the sign through the medium of some translator or sign-interpreting agency (and need not be just human agency).[11] This suggests that the translation is at once a *product*, the result of some *process* (that is, the process of *semeiosis* itself; cf. CP 5.484), which has some *effect* on the translator: " . . . the essential effect upon the interpreter [is] brought about by the semeiosis of the sign . . . " (CP 5.484). This understanding reconciles the various definitions of the interpretant, each of which stresses one of these aspects of the interpretant. Thus Peirce often defines the interpretant in terms of its "proper significate effect" on the interpreter (CP 5.473, 5.475, 2.228, 8.191). Often it is understood as the product of such a process (semiosis) (CP 4.536; cf. CP 5.484), that is, as simply another sign which results from other signs (CP 2.228, 8.191). But also it is understood as the process itself, that is, as a *rule* of sign translation (cf. CP 5.484, 5.483).

There are several different divisions which Peirce gives to the interpretant: one of the primary divisions is the *immediate, dynamic*, and *final* (CP 8.314, MS 339d: 546–547, LW 109–111); the immediate interpretant is sometimes called *felt* (CP 8.369), *naive* (MS 499: 47), or *rogate* (MS 499: 47); the dynamic interpretant is also called the *middle* interpretant (NEM 4: 318); the final interpretant is sometimes called *eventual* (CP 8.372), *normal* (CP 8.343), or *ultimate* (CP 8.314). Another important division is among the *emotional, energetic*, and *logical* (CP 5.475–476, MS 318: 35–37), and the logical is subdivided into *first, lower*, and *higher second, third*, and *ultimate* (MS 318: 169–171). Other divisions include the *intentional, effectual*, and *communicational* (LW 196); *destinate, effective, explicit* (LW 84).

There is some controversy concerning how these various types are to be related,[12] but a safe interpretation suggests a relation among them analogous to the way in which Peirce's categories are articulated. Firstness, secondness, and thirdness are thought to be the most comprehensive classification of the categories; the other divisions can be thought of as species of these comprehensive categories, but as seen from a certain perspective or context. Thus monad, dyad, and triad are, respectively, species of firstness, secondness, and thirdness, but in regard to formal relations; quality, fact, and law are metaphysical categories that correspond, respectively, to the comprehensive ones. Similarly, the most comprehensive division of interpretants might be considered that of immediate, dynamic, and final, while the emotional, energetic, and logical classification could be thought of as the matter of interpretants in regard to human or humanlike agency, that is, to agencies capable of feeling and deliberate or self-controlled conduct; the division of intentional, effectual, and communicational has special application to semeioses that involve communication, while the destinate, effective, explicit looks at the interpretant in regard to its ontological status as a possible, actual, or necessitant.

First, let's consider the characteristics of the most comprehensive classification: immediate, dynamic, and final. Keeping in mind that the interpretant can be viewed as process, product, and effect, then the immediate interpretant can be thought of as the "total unanalyzed effect" that the sign is intentionally designed to produce or might naturally produce (LW 110), "the immediate pertinent possible effect in its unanalyzed primitive entirety" (MS 339d: 546). It can also be understood as the process which allows the interpreting agency to interpret its sign as interpretable as such (LW 110). As a product, it would include any sort of firstness, including the quality involved in a feeling, vague impressions, qualities, the *idea* of an effort (and not the effort itself), or the *idea* of a general type (MS 339d: 546). Its cousin is the emotional interpretant, which for any interpreting agency capable of emotion or feeling is precisely that initial feeling produced by the sign (CP 5.475). Thus the overall feeling one is left with after listening to Beethoven's Seventh Symphony may be considered the immediate interpretant of the sign taken as a whole (cf. CP 5.475); so too may the impression upon viewing the *Mona Lisa* for the first time, a certain immediate dislike one has of someone first met, or the sense that there is something significant in an intentionally arranged set of stones in the middle of the forest.

The dynamic interpretant, on the other hand, consists in the *direct* or *actual* effect produced by a sign upon some interpreting agency (LW 110, CP 4.536, MS 339d: 546); "it is whatever interpretation any mind actually makes of a sign" (CP 8.315). Its product would belong to the category of secondness, such as actions, events, or singularly produced ideas (MS 339d: 546). The dynamic interpretant has both an active and a passive modality, for example, a daydream may serve as a sign which actively produces an ambition in a young person (CP 8.315), while the shock of surprise might be seen as a more passively determined dynamic interpretant (CP 8.315). The cousin of the dynamic interpretant is the energetic interpretant, which is the effect of exertion any sign has on an interpreting agency (CP 5.475). This exertion can be either physical or mental (CP 5.475). Thus a sign might provoke one into thought or cause one to rise from his seat. A command might lead directly to an action (CP 5.475, MS 292: 15), or a loud voice might make one jump. Peirce makes it clear that the dynamic and the energetic interpretants cannot harbor the meaning of the sign (CP 5.475), only its singular effects. However, energetic interpretants are integral to the establishment of logical interpretants (CP 5.476), just as emotional ones are integral to the establishment of energetic interpretants (CP 5.475), in the sense that the higher-order interpretants are developed through the mediation of the lower ones (CP 5.475).

The final interpretant is any rulelike or lawlike effect a sign has on any interpreting agency (LW 110). It is, as Peirce writes, "the ultimate effect of the sign, so far as it is intended or destined, from the character of the sign, being more or less of a habitual and formal nature . . ." (MS 339d: 547). Its products will be thirds, such as laws, habits, dispositions, and regularities; its cousin is the logical interpretant.[13] The logical interpretant can be thought of as the conceptual import, the meaning of the sign (CP 5.475), understood as the "would-be" of the sign, as Peirce suggests (CP 5.482), that is, the *expression* (CP 5.491) of the generalizable outcome of the sign (CP 5.483). The final or ultimate logical interpretant, on the other hand, is the habit of interpretation or the habit of action which interpretation of the sign engenders (CP 5.491, 5.486): "the deliberately formed, self-analyzing habit . . . is the living definition, the veritable and final logical interpretant" (CP 5.491). Thus, according to Peirce, the most perfect account of a concept, or any sign, consists "in a description of the habit which the concept is calculated to produce" (CP 5.491), which, of course, is the essence of the pragmatic maxim: "consider what effects, that might conceivably have practical bearings, we conceive the object of our conception to have. Then, our conception of these effects is the whole of our conception of the object" (CP 5.402).

Generally speaking, the final interpretant can be understood as the means by which a sign becomes connected or interrelated into a system of signs, that is, translated "into another system of signs" (CP 4.127). "A system," according to Peirce, "is a set of objects comprising all that stand to one another in a group of connected relations" (CP 4.5). Signs become interrelated in such a way as to create certain generalizable effects, that is, the systematic translation of a sign. Peirce articulates this idea from different aspects, each of which allows a certain appreciation of the interpretant. On the one hand, the final interpretant(s), as a product(s) of sign translation, could be understood as the state of *information* which the sign (in its relation to other signs) affords. The status of the information would change as the system evolves. On the other hand, the final interpretant, viewed from the perspective of a process, can be understood as the rule(s) of such translation, which for Peirce, is primarily in terms of the various types of *inference* or reasoning, namely, abduction, deduction, and induction (to be discussed in chapter 3). These provide the means by which the system of signs grows, evolves, and develops. Finally, as an effect, the final interpretant determines certain *habits of conduct* for sign-interpreting agencies incorporated into the system of signs, the way in which signs become the lived experience of such agencies. The aspects are interrelated: information changes as inferences expand or complicate the system, while the information of the system results in significant changes in the conduct of the sign-interpreting agencies; the conduct of interpreting agencies, in turn, feeds the system into a certain direction based on the patterns of inference operative in the system. The final interpretant is the full import of the sign: it is a translation of the sign which results in information by means of rules of inference which has, coordinately, a certain effect on sign-interpreting agencies. Each of these aspects of the interpretant—information, inference, and habits of conduct—is analyzed in some detail by Peirce.

Information,[14] according to Peirce, can be understood as the coordination of the sense and reference, the connotation and denotation, of the sign[15] (what Peirce calls its depth and breadth). The relation between depth and breadth, sense and reference, is mediated by information.[16] Signs refer by means of having a sense relative to a state of information, and the sense of the sign can only be specified by means of reference, relative to a state of information.[17] As Peirce writes,

> . . . the dyadic relations of logical breadth and depth, often called denotation and connotation, have played a great part in logical discussion, but these take their origin in the triadic relation between sign, its object and its interpretant sign; and furthermore, the list appears as a dichotomy owing to the limitation of the field of thought, which forgets that concepts grow, and there is the third respect in which they may differ, depending on the state of knowledge, or amount of information. (CP 3.608)

The notions of depth and breadth are refined by Peirce in the following way. The *essential depth* of a sign is all the qualities or characteristics that are predicated of it simply by means of its definition, or general, conventional understanding (CP 2.410). The *essential breadth*, on the other hand, is all those things to which, according to its very meaning, the sign refers. The term "human being" has a dictionary meaning, and refers to whatever satisfies that definition in a vague and general way. Peirce claims that the essential depth and breadth of a sign do not really give us information in the strict sense of the term, but instead a sort of "verbal knowledge" (MS 664: 20): "I do not call the knowledge that a person known to be a woman is an adult, nor the knowledge that a corpse is not a woman, by the name 'information,' because the word 'woman' *means* a living adult human being having, or having had, female sexuality" (MS 664: 20). The *informed depth* of a sign is the depth of the sign relative to an actual state of information (CP 2.408); it is the attribution of depth to certain objects which we know to have those attributions. Put simply, it is what we can ascribe truthfully to an object or a class of objects given our present state of knowledge. We may know that John, who is a human being, has certain cortical functions not found in any other mammal. Correlatively, the *informed breadth* of a sign is all those objects to which the information refers (CP 2.407). Finally, the *substantial depth* of a sign is the collection of meaning which can be assigned to it in a state of complete information or absolute truth (CP 2.413); it would involve the complete determination of the sign. The *substantial breadth* is all that to which the substantial depth refers (CP 2.414).

Peirce defines information as the quantity of the interpretant (W 1: 465). Information is a dimension of meaning achieved in the systematic intersection (or the area) of the sign's breadth and depth (CP 2.419). Since information is established in the coordination of depth and breadth, it is primarily expressed propositionally. Granted that the essential depth and breadth of signs understood as terms can provide us with some information (cf. CP 2.250), that is, "verbal knowledge," still the primary expression of information is found in the proposition. This is precisely because the proposition, understood as the connection or "identity" of a subject term with a predicate term (CP 2.316), *is* the coordination of depth and breadth of those terms. If we learn that S is P, then as a general rule the depth of S is increased and the breadth of P is increased (CP 2.419). To learn that arsenic is poisonous claims, in effect, that the informed depth of arsenic is increased, while the informed breadth of poisonous things is increased. The proposition extends the breadth and depth of terms by showing that the breadth of a depth term and the depth of a breadth term now extend to another term not previously related to it. In a proposition, generally expressed as "S is P," the copula indicates the work of the interpretant, for it connects two diverse terms, which has the effect of producing information (W 3: 97): "every addition to the information which is encased in a term results in making some term equivalent to that term" (W 1: 464). "Indeed, the process of getting an equivalent for a term, is an identity of two terms previously diverse. . . . Each of these equivalents is the explication of what there is wrapt up in the primary. . . . I call them the interpretant of the term. And the quantity of these interpretants I term the information or implication of the term" (W 1: 464–465).

The information that is expressed in the proposition does not arrive ex nihilo but is the accomplishment of previous translations of signs understood as inferences. Any proposition can be understood as the conclusion of some argument or inference (CP 5.279, 2.253). If the final interpretant can be understood, at least in one respect, as the ordered, lawlike, and general systematic expansion of signs, that is, the organization of information pertaining to the sign, the primary means by which such organization is established is through inference and reasoning in general: "the illative [i.e., inferential] relation is the primary and paramount semiotic relation" (CP 2.444n1). Inference serves to expand and increase the level of information in the system of signs:

> The effect of an addition to our knowledge is to make one term predicable of another which was not so before to our knowledge. And it thus at once increases the known depth of the subject term, and the known breadth of the predicate term without any decrease of either of these quantities, so that in the increase of knowledge, the known breadth and depth of terms are constantly increasing and the sum of the breadths and depths in either product, if you please, will measure the extent to which investigation has been pushed. (W 3: 89)

Inferences are either explicative or ampliative. The first sort—which is exemplified by deduction—function to complicate the system rather than expand it, mainly by showing implicit connections that exist among connections made already in the existing state of information. As Peirce says, deduction does not involve a change of information, although it serves to increase the depth and breadth of signs (CP 2.423, 5.279). On the other hand, through ampliative reasoning—exemplified by abduction and induction—the information in the system of signs is expanded in new ways, the first by developing hypotheses, the second by confirming them. For this reason, a crucial part of semeiotic is the study of proper reasoning, and so critical logic plays a vital role in this matter (an issue dealt with in chapter 3).

If information is expressed propositionally and is the result of a process of inference, still its final import lies elsewhere: " . . . of the myriads of forms into which a proposition may be translated, what is that one which is to be called its very meaning? It is, according to the pragmaticist, that form in which the proposition becomes applicable to human conduct . . . " (CP 5.427). It appears that the highest expression of the final interpretant of a sign (or a system of signs), that is, the translation of a sign, is found in terms of the effects—primarily in terms of the sorts of habits of conduct established in the interpreting agencies integral to that system of signs. This is derived from the essence of the pragmatic maxim, which argues that the import of the sign is established in its generalizable effects (cf. CP 5.402), or, in this case, the effect on such interpreters of signs: "it is to conceptions of deliberate conduct that Pragmaticism would trace the intellectual purport of symbols . . . " (CP 5.442); "the being of a symbol consists in the real fact that something surely will be experienced if certain conditions be satisfied. Namely, it will influence the thought and conduct of its interpreter" (CP 4.447). The information provided by the system of signs, and the very process of reasoning by which such information is acquired, will affect interpreting agencies accordingly. If the information is true, the reasoning involved valid, then the effect in such a system, according to Peirce, is "that it seems to make thought and conduct rational and enables us to predict the future" (CP 4.448); it establishes a form of "concrete reasonableness." We assume, conversely, that false or distorted information and invalid forms of reasoning produce contrary habits of conduct, or the inability to form such habits at all. For this reason, critical logic—which hopes to establish an account of good reasoning—becomes all the more critical.

The Triadic Relation (the Triadic Condition)

The fourth formal condition, which insists on the triadic interrelation of sign, object, and interpretant, accounts for the action of the sign, that is, semeiosis. Peirce defines the latter as "an act, or influence, which is, or involves, a cooperation of three subjects, such as a sign, its object and its interpretant, this tri-relative influence not being in any way resolvable into acts between pairs" (CP 5.484). Semeiosis is not the additive or mechanical reproduction of the relations between sign-object and sign-interpretant and object-interpretant, but the three form an indissoluble bond, not reducible to any kind of dyadic relation (see figure 2).[18]

The irreducible quality of triadic relations is illustrated by Peirce in two analogies, that of giving and that of intentional action:

> Analyze for instance the relation involved in "A gives B to C." Now what is giving? It does not consist in A's putting B away from him and C's subsequently taking B up. It is not necessary that any material transfer should take place. It consists in A's making C the possessor according to Law. There must be some kind of law before there can be any kind of giving—be it but the law of the strongest. (CP 8.331)

The act of giving suggests a coherence between three phases: "Here are three pairs. A parts with B, C receives B, A enriches C. But these three dual facts taken together do not make up the triple fact which consists in this,

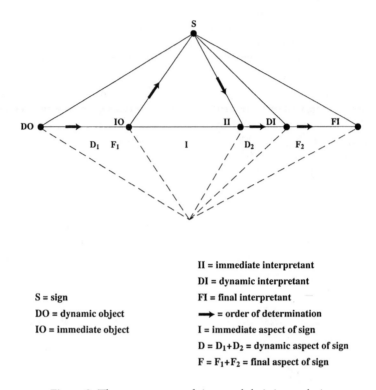

II = immediate interpretant

DI = dynamic interpretant

S = sign   FI = final interpretant

DO = dynamic object   ➝ = order of determination

IO = immediate object   I = immediate aspect of sign

D = $D_1 + D_2$ = dynamic aspect of sign

F = $F_1 + F_2$ = final aspect of sign

Figure 2. The components of signs and their interrelation.

that A parts with B, C receives B, and A enriches C, *all in one act*" (NEM 4: 307).

As opposed to triadic relations, dyadic relations can be analyzed into pair relations, e.g., as in a series of causal relations (CP 5.472–473).[19] An event A may produce an event B by brute force, and B may in turn produce by brute force an event C; but the fact that the event C is about to be produced by B has no influence at all upon the production of B by A. This is so since the action of B in producing C is a contingent event at the time B is produced. In other words, B is not produced in order to produce C, but *because* B was produced by A, then C *could be* produced by B. On the other hand, in a triadic relation A produces B *as a means to* the production of C. B is produced because it is likely to produce C, not because it was produced by A.[20] The intentional description of an action involves reference to the triadic relation between intention, result, and action and cannot be reduced to a series of causal relations between the phases of the action. Intentional behavior (as distinct from intentionality generally) is thus analogous to semeiosis in this respect: goal, means, and action correspond, respectively, to object, interpretant, and sign. The goal (object) determines the action relative to the means; the means are determined relative to the goal, and the action realizes the goal in terms of the means. Peirce makes a similar analogy (NEM 4: 254).[21]

Attenuation to the triadic condition generates three basic types of semeioses.[22] Peirce does not explicitly name them except to distinguish them as either genuinely or degenerately triadic.[23] Since the triadic condition is marked by intentionality and purposiveness (MS 292: 13, 339D: 664), we might, for the sake of convenience, distinguish them on the basis of different sorts of goal-directedness.[24] In that case, the first sort of triadic relation might be called *teleological* (implying that the intentionality of the system is deliberate); the second, *teleonomic* (implying that the intentionality of the process is indurated);[25] and the third, *mechanical* (or *computational*—indicating dyadically produced interpretation).

Teleological semeiosy is capable of generating *genuine* signs, i.e., conventional symbols (after all, a "purpose is precisely the interpretant of a symbol" (NEM 4: 244; cf. NEM 4: 254, 4: 261). In these cases the interpretation is triadically produced. This must involve mind in its fullest sense, that is, mentality capable of convention (cf. CP 4.551). The human brain is, for example, capable of making connections between signs and objects not naturally or causally established. As Peirce writes, "whether the interpretant be necessarily a triadic result is a question of words, that is, of how we limit the extension of the term 'sign'; but it seems to me convenient to make the triadic production of the interpretant essential to a 'sign'" (CP 5.473).

The semeiosy is teleonomic if the interpretant is triadically produced but not conventionally established. Rather than mind in its fullest sense, the interpretant is bound up with what Peirce calls a *quasi-mind* (CP 4.551, NEM 4: 318), which is clearly not restricted to the human cortex (NEM 4: 318). The triadic character of the semeiosy is defined by natural dispositions. Animal communication and sign use are typical of these sorts of semeiosy, although they are found at certain levels of human semeiosy as well.[26] The signs generated in this sort of process are not genuine ones but are signs in the *broad* sense of the term. Here the interpretation of signs is not automatic; it does vary; it grows and exhibits correction. But nonetheless the interpretation has its basis in a naturally indurated habit rather than deliberate self-control. As Peirce writes, "thought is not necessarily connected with a brain. It appears in the work of bees, of crystals, and throughout the purely physical world . . . " (CP 4.551). One might say that the habit of interpretation, the logical interpretant, is already operative and not deliberately formed; corrections to the habits evolve over time but are not highly influenced by conscious self-correction.

Mechanical semeiosy seems to be capable of generating what Peirce calls a *quasi-sign* (CP 5.473). In this case the interpretant is dyadically produced, that is, the interpreting agency is caused in a mechanical way to respond to the sign without alteration or correction to that program. There is little inherent development or correction in these sorts of processes unless made from some external source; goals are automatically predetermined or set by agencies external to the system. Peirce gives the example of a thermostatic system and a Jacquard loom (a weaving machine with an automatic weaving head) (CP 5.473), and so we assume this analysis would apply to most, if not all, cybernetic or servomechanisms.

The Typology of Signs

In addition to disclosing the formal conditions of a sign, semeiotic grammar is interested in describing the various classes or types of signs. This is the job of sign *typology*. By typology, Peirce means the business of discerning a type (or natural class; cf. CP 1.203 ff.), whose description captures, generally, the ways in which the things which belong to it behave in an analogous way (cf. CP 1.223); in this context it is the business of sign *division*. Sign *classification*, on the other hand, is the broad organization of these types (or natural classes) by means of a systematic plan or idea that intends to demonstrate the affinity, dependence, or interdependence of the types (cf. CP 1.180).

Peirce develops four different typologies, which might be called the *original*, the *interim*, the *expanded*, and the *final*.[27] The original appears in "On a New List of Categories" (CP 1.545–1.567). According to this typology,[28] there are three kinds of signs: icons (or likenesses), indices, and symbols (CP 1.558). Symbols are further divided into terms, propositions, and arguments (CP 1.559); arguments are further subdivided into deduction, hypothesis (later, abduction), and induction (CP 1.559). This trichotomous aspect of signs is more fully articulated in 1903 in the interim typology. Instead of one trichotomy which is subdivided as in the original, the interim classification treats terms, propositions, and arguments (now called rhemes, dicents, and arguments) as a separate trichotomy from symbols (and icons and indices). Arguments are still subdivided into deduction, abduction, and induction. Peirce then adds a third trichotomy, namely, the sign considered in itself. The interim typology also engages in genuine sign classification for the first time. In the following year, Peirce presents the expanded version of the 1903 typology (cf. LW 22–36). Not only does it include the three trichotomies of the 1903 division, but on the basis of his distinction between the dynamic and immediate object and his division of interpretants into immediate, dynamic, and final, there are now three additional trichotomies: the relation of the sign to the immediate object, the appeal of the sign to its dynamic interpretant, and the relation of the sign to its immediate interpretant. The final typology adds four new trichotomies, bringing the total to ten.[29] However, although the final typology is an interesting experiment, it is rather undeveloped and tentative in Peirce. For this reason, and for the reason that the most detailed classification of signs is associated with the interim typology, focus on the 1903 typology might be the most fruitful.

Using the interim typology, any sign can be analyzed in three aspects which correspond to the first three formal conditions of the sign: the sign qua sign, that is, the sign in regard to its ground; the sign in regard to its object; and the sign in regard to its interpretant. Following the logic here, the first—the aspect of sign qua sign—might be called the sign's *presentative* character (cf. CP 1.313 for a hint of this idea in Peirce); the second, the relation of sign to object, might be called its *representative* character; and the third, the sign's relation to its interpretant, its *interpretative* character (or what Peirce sometimes called its *signification*; cf. CP 8.378).

The Typology of Signs in Regard to Their Presentative Character

The presentative character of the sign is a certain feature which the sign has qua object (or existent) which forms the basis of its *capacity* as a sign to represent its object, that is, serves as the ground of the sign. The presentative character of the sign, then, forms the basis of its representative character. A star, for example, may serve as a sign in many capacities because of its brightness, or the fact that it appears only at night, or because it seems to point toward a certain direction, or because of its accumulated historical and conventional senses. In the first case, the presentative character of the sign involves its qualitative characteristics. For example, if something is red and for that reason becomes a sign, then in that regard it is called a *qualisign* (CP 2.244) (also called a *tone* [CP 4.537], *tuone* [MS 339d: 533–534], or *potisign* [CP 8.344]). But if the presentative character of the sign is in terms of its existential qualities, it is called a *sinsign* (CP 2.245) (also called a *token* [CP 4.537] or *actisign* [CP 8.344]). When the red buzzer flashes and sounds *now*, it makes it a sign for that reason, that is, its instantiation is the determining feature for its representative capability. In terms of its presentative quality, when a sign is a *sinsign* it acts primarily through its singularity, its temporality, or its unique location. Finally, a third characteristic which provides the capacity for a sign to represent is any conventional, dispositional, or lawlike feature it may have acquired. The fact that red is often used conventionally to signal danger or to be a warning helps give the red light a certain capacity to represent its object. In this case the sign is called a *legisign* (CP 2.246) (or a *type* [CP 4.537] or *famisign* [CP 8.344]).

A sign can have all three presentative characteristics, although usually only one predominates. There is also a certain sort of hierarchy among these characteristics. A quality is always embodied in a singularity, but if the quality is the predominant aspect of the sign, then it is a qualisign. Every singularity has some quality (CP 2.245), but when it is the bare fact of its singularity that counts the most, then it is a sinsign. A generality is always embodied in a singularity (CP 2.246) which has a certain quality, but when it is its generality that predominates, then it is a legisign. For example, the word THE is a legisign because it primarily signifies through its conventionality. Granted that THE is singular, it is not so much its singularity that makes it a sign, since any *replica* (CP 2.246) (or *token*)[30] of THE would have the same effect. Although the qualities of THE (its shape and form) are essential to recognize it as the sign that it is, it is not primarily the qualities that it has which make it a sign; rather it is the fact that the qualities have been conventionalized (cf. MS 280: 81). As Peirce says, "it consists in the really working general rule that three such patches seen by a person who knows English will affect his conduct and thoughts according to a rule" (CP 4.448; cf. also CP 4.432). One could imagine the meaning of THE represented by some other shape or form, as is clear when we use another language. DAS is roughly equivalent to THE, and so it is not the quality of the sign that makes it what it is, although it must have some quality. Both THE and DAS refer to the same object but do not have the same qualities.

Something does not have to be conventional to be a legisign, so long as it has some lawlike, habitual, or dispositional characteristic. Thus a bird song might be considered from one aspect as a legisign, since a particular song sung by a bird of the species (in regard to mating, let's say) is nearly identical to any other but manages to evoke, potentially, the same response.

The Typology of Signs in Regard to Their Representative Character

The presentative character of a sign is its characteristic pre-scinded from any relation it has to its object; the representative character of the sign, on the other hand, concerns the *relation* or *correlation* between sign and object. The representative character of a sign (the division of signs probably most familiar to many readers), then, concerns the manner in which a sign correlates with its object and so establishes itself as a representation of that object. In this regard it uses the presentative characteristics or the ground of the sign to establish that correlation, and it does this in three essential ways. If the presentative characteristics of the sign are *similar* to the object and it thereby establishes its correlation with that object primarily by that means, then the sign is called an *icon*. If, on the other hand, the presentative characteristics of the sign are *contiguous* with the object and it thereby establishes its correlation with that object primarily by that means, then the sign is called an *index*. Finally, if the sign establishes its correlation with an object primarily through the conventional, natural, or lawlike presentational characteristics of a sign, then the sign becomes a *symbol*.

An *icon* (CP 2.247, 2.276) (also called a *likeness* [CP 1.558] or more strictly a *hypoicon*)[31] correlates with its object because the sign's qualities are similar to the object's characteristics. A photograph or portrait of a person is an icon because the photo has many features which the original face has. An icon can be similar to its object by the fact that it partakes of or shares the same qualities with its object. For example, the rose is red and the painting of a rose is red; in that case it is called an *image* (CP 2.277). In this regard, Peirce suggests, an icon represents "by virtue of characters which belong to it in itself as a sensible object, and which it would possess just the same were there no object in nature that it resembled, and though it never were interpreted as a sign" (CP 2.447). An icon can also be similar to its object when the relations among the elements in the sign are isomorphic to relations among elements in the object. The standard example of this would be that of map to terrain; in that case it is called a *diagram* (CP 2.277). Analogies would also be good examples of diagrams, since they show a parallel between relations in one thing to relations in another: A is to B as C is to D. A sign is also an icon when the representative character of a sign is represented by showing a parallel to the representative character of another sign. In that case it is called a *metaphor* (CP 2.277). For example, "Before he could hear the shot, he fell, his body a spilled vessel of wine." The metaphor conveys the *sense* of the disposition of the body as blood flows from a wound by showing it parallel to the disposition of a spilled bottle of wine.[32] So the metaphor is not an analogy (and hence a diagram), since it doesn't aim to show a similarity in relations between two things but to represent the *representative character* of one thing *by means of* another thing which has similarity to the first in a certain respect.

A sign may represent its object not only by means of similarity but also by contiguity with its object. In that case it is called an *index* (CP 2.248). It is the sign's singularity, its spatial or temporal location, its "here and now" vis-à-vis the object, rather than any qualities that it has, which contributes to making it an index (CP 4.56). Consequently, it is the sign's contiguity with its object that is the essential feature of an index (CP 2.248), although Peirce indicates other important features.[33] The contiguity can be of basically three different sorts. It can be *deictic* (or *referential*; cf. CP 2.283), in the sense that there is a perception of direct continuity between the sign and its object; for example, as the way in which a pointing finger draws an imaginary line to the object it refers to (CP 2.305), or the way in which a demonstrative pronoun, given its specific utterance, will indicate which object is referred to (cf. CP 4.158, 2.287, 3.361, 6.338). These types of indices are sometimes called *designatives* by Peirce (CP 8.368n). It can also be *causal* (or *existential*; cf. CP 2.283), such that the index is caused by the object it represents (CP 4.531); an example would be the way in which the wind pushes a windvane into a certain pointing position (CP 2.286). These types are also sometimes called *reagents* by Peirce (CP 8.368n). Finally, the index may result from an initial *labeling*, as a proper name becomes associated with someone (cf. CP 2.329) or as in the case of putting a letter beneath a diagram (CP 2.285, 3.361).

In addition to this essential characteristic of contiguity, Peirce also emphasizes that a genuine index involves individuals (as opposed to types, collections, and generals) (CP 2.283). For that reason an index does not really assert anything about the object it represents, so much as it shows or exhibits that object (CP 3.361). However, Peirce emphasizes that this exhibition of the object can lead to different results depending on whether the index is a designative or a reagent. In the first case, the index only serves to stand for the object it represents, as "A" may stand for the first person in a contract; generally a designative only announces the object, as a demonstrative pronoun does. A proper name cannot really provide us any information about the object it represents (unless it has an iconic aspect to it, e.g., Long John or Patcheye). However, a reagent, given the causal connection, can serve as the basis for ascertaining facts concerning its object, as a weathervane can tell us something about the direction of the wind. Also, in showing or exhibiting the object, it often does so by means of gaining the attention of the interpreter (CP 2.357, 3.434, 2.256, 2.259, 2.336), like the rap on a door.

In addition to similarity and contiguity, a sign may represent its object by means of some conventional, habitual, dispositional, or lawlike relation, in which case it is called a *symbol*. "A symbol is a representamen whose special significance or fitness to represent just what it does represent lies in nothing but the very fact of there being a habit, disposition, or other effective general rule that it will be so interpreted" (CP 4.447). The habit or general rule involved may be natural (CP 2.307) or "in-born" (CP 2.297), or it may be "acquired" (CP 2.297), that is, conventional (CP 2.307).[34] In both cases, however, the characteristic of the symbol is the same, such that, predominantly speaking, there is no similarity or contiguity between the presentative character of the sign and the object it represents, although, as Peirce argues, the symbol must include iconic and indexical elements at some level (CP 2.294–2.295). The symbol is connected with its object "by virtue of the idea of the symbol-using mind, without which no such connection would exist" (CP 2.299). It is a sign "which is constituted a sign merely or mainly by the fact that it is used and understood as such . . . and without regard to the motives which originally governed its selection" (CP 2.307). As an example of what might be called a *natural* symbol, when the dog wags its tail as a gesture of friendliness, there appears to be no similarity (or motivation in Saussure's sense) between the movement, direction, and velocity of the tail and the state of friendliness; yet the gesture is a natural indurated habit for most species of dogs. Words are exemplary forms of conventional symbols, according to Peirce (CP 2.292). The word "man" represents what it does by the fact that it is a general mode of succession of three sounds or signs of sounds established through a habit or acquired law, which will cause replicas of it to be interpreted as meaning a man or men (CP 2.292). "The word and its meaning are both general rules . . . " (CP 2.292). So, in general, the symbol is a sign precisely because it is interpreted or used as such (CP 2.307, 2.292, 4.448):

> a chalk mark is like a line though nobody uses it as a sign; a weathercock turns with the wind, whether anybody notices it or not. But the word "man" has no particular relation to men unless it be recognized as being so related. That is not only what constitutes it a sign, but what gives it the peculiar relation to its object which makes it significant of that particular object. (L 75)

Thus the symbol "is a sign which would lose the character which renders it a sign if there were no interpretant" (CP 2.304). It is unlike the icon, "which would possess the character which renders it significant, even though its object had no existence," but like the index, which is a sign "which would, at once, lose the character which makes it a sign if its object were removed" (CP 2.304).

Because the symbol can only act through a law or habit, it is "itself a general type" (CP 2.249). As such it acts through replicas or instances of itself: "now that which is general has its being in the instances which it will determine" (CP 2.249). The symbol "is a law, or regularity of the indefinite future . . . and is embodied in individuals, and prescribes some of their qualities" (CP 2.293). The object it refers to is also of a general kind usually (CP 2.249), in which case it is called a *genuine* symbol (CP 2.293), and so has a general meaning. If the object of the symbol is an existent individual, for example, "moon," then it is called a *singular* symbol; if the object of the symbol is some character or quality, simply, then it is called an *abstract* symbol.

The Typology of Signs in Regard to Their Interpretative Power

In addition to its presentative character and its representative capacity, the sign also has an interpretative power (CP 1.542). This is the sign's power to direct or determine its interpretants toward a certain focus in the interpretation of its object. If a sign is a *rheme* (alternately called *seme*; CP 4.538), it will have a tendency to determine the interpretant to focus on the qualitative characteristics of the sign rather than on any existential or lawlike properties it might have. Peirce's typical example of a rheme is a term (such as "human being") (CP 8.337), or the predicate of a proposition (CP 4.438 ff.) (more specifically the proposition absent any referring subject). There are various types of terms (sometimes called *cyrioids* or *singular quantities*; CP 5.450) according to Peirce, including proper names, demonstratives, personal and relative pronouns, abstract and common nouns. The common noun or term "human being" in and of itself suggests to human interpreters familiar with the English language the various characteristics which the term connotes, rather than the application or indication of the term as representing or referring to a particular object. These characteristics might be embodied in some possible object, but the sign itself does not indicate what object that might be. In this case the reference of a seme is excessively vague (CP 4.539). As Peirce writes, the "word dog—meaning *some dog*; implies the knowledge there is some dog, but it remains indefinite. The *Interpretant* is the somewhat indefinite *idea* of the characters that the 'some dog' referred to has . . . " (MS 854: 2). Because of the indefiniteness of the rheme, it is neither true nor false; it does not make an assertion[35] about something or provide information (although it provides some; CP 2.250), but simply exhibits characteristics as such. One could say that for a rheme its interpretation will be directed more toward the sense, the connotation or depth, of the sign than toward its reference, its denotation or breadth. In a rheme there is an indefiniteness of breadth (CP 4.543), and its object is excessively vague (CP 4.539). But although there is impetus toward the depth of the sign, there is certainly an element of interpretation concerned with the breadth in every rheme (cf. CP 2.341), but the breadth is more of a possibility or a product of the imagination than actual (CP 2.250, 2.341). One might say that the rheme is a sign whose depth is seeking breadth; it leaves "its Object, and *a fortiori* its Interpretant, to be what it may" (CP 2.95).

Understood on the model of terms, rhemes can be subdivided into *medadic* rhema, which are terms plain and simple; *monadic* rhema, such as "_____ is good"; *dyadic* rhema, such as "_____ loves _____"; and *triadic* rhema, such as "God gives _____ to _____" (CP 4.438).

A *dicent* (alternately called a *pheme*; CP 4.538) connects sense with reference, depth with breadth, that is, connects rhemes into a higher interpretive organization, and so its interpretation allows one (or forces one) to ascertain that a certain characteristic is true of a certain object, that is, it determines the interpretant toward the information in the sign: "I define a dicent as a sign represented in its signified interpretant as if it were in a Real Relation to its Object" (LW 34). The focus of the interpretation is on the claim that this object has this characteristic, and so the focus is the correlation of depth with breadth. The paradigm of the dicent for Peirce, then, is the proposition (CP 2.309 ff.), which does precisely this through the connection of a predicate with a subject. The proposition "John is a human being" says, for example, of this object that it is a human being, so its interpretation is directed to the correlation of depth and breadth, or sense and reference, to determine the extent of objects which have the characteristics indicated in the predicate, on the one hand, and to augment the depth of objects referred to by ascribing those predicates to them, on the other.

As mentioned earlier, every proposition according to Peirce involves a subject and predicate, and that is the basic means by which a proposition can convey information. But depending on other characteristics of propositions, such as their modality, quality, quantity, and form, the sort of information conveyed will differ. Thus Peirce classifies propositions into several types, based on these differences, and in ways which are standard in modern logical classifications. The first division is between modal propositions, those that articulate the possible, impossible, contingent, or necessary, and *de inesse*, that is, those which concern only the existing state of things (such as "John is a human being"; CP 2.323, 2.382). In addition, the subject of a proposition can be either singular, general, or abstract (CP 2.324), corresponding to the three subtypes of symbols, for example, "moon," "human being," and "red," respectively. The general, in turn, is subdivided into either universal or particular (CP 2.324, 2.271): "Some human beings are philosophers" would be an example of the latter, while "All philosophers are wise" would be an example of the former. Propositions can also be divided by form into hypothetical, categorical, and relative (CP 2.325), although Peirce, like most modern logicians, sees no difference between hypothetical and categorical propositions. Thus "If p, then q," which is hypothetical, translates the logical sense of "All p is q." The relative proposition is concerned with the identity of more than one individual (CP 2.271), such as "John loves Mary." Propositions can also be distinguished in terms of their quality, either affirmative or negative, for example, "All philosophers live well" and "No philosopher is happy."[36]

An *argument* (alternately called a *delome*; CP 4.538) is a sign whose interpretation is directed to the systematic, inferential, or lawlike connection with other signs; it determines the interpretant toward the inferential form or rulelike character of the sign. It is, as Peirce says, a "sign which, for its Interpretant, is a sign of law" (CP 2.252). The paradigm of the argument for Peirce is its namesake, the argument (CP 2.253).

Just as the proposition or dicent incorporates rhemes or terms into a higher interpretant, so arguments incorporate dicents or propositions into a higher interpretant. Consider for a moment the example of a typical syllogistic argument: "All human beings are mammals. All mammals are vertebrates. Therefore all human beings are vertebrates." In the argument, the propositions which serve as premises not only convey their own particular information but lead to another piece of information not stated by either premise but, of course, expressed by the proposition in the conclusion. On one hand the interpretant of the argument is the conclusion, understood as product of the argument (CP 2.95, 2.253). On the other hand, understood as a process, the interpretant is the rule of inference, or leading principle, in the argument (CP 2.263, 4.375). Finally, understood as effect, the interpretant of the argument "has the Form of tending to act upon the Interpreter through his own self-control, representing a process of change in thoughts or signs, as if to induce this change in the Interpreter" (CP 4.538). In all three senses of the interpretant, the argument as sign determines the interpretant towards the habitual, rulelike character of the sign.

By analogy, just as the proposition provides different types of information depending on its type, so an argument will have different effects on interpreters and different types of rulelike inferences, depending on the type of argument it is. For Peirce there are three basic types of arguments: abduction, deduction, and induction. Since these will be analyzed in some detail in the next chapter, an outline of their general characteristics might be more appropriate here. Deductive arguments are explicative forms of inference, in the sense that they make explicit what is implicit among systematic connections of signs, given the current state of information for that system. Deductions simply show what is already there but not noticed, so to speak. Its prototypical form is the transitive relation (CP 5.279): "S is M. M is P. Therefore, S is P." Both induction and abduction on the other hand are ampliative types of inferences, in the sense that they expand the amount of information in the system of signs. Abduction, especially in Peirce's later analysis of this form of reasoning, concerns the introduction or discovery of possibly new propositions or hypotheses, based on anomalous or surprising events generated from the received information of the system of signs (cf. CP 2.624). Finally, induction, generally speaking, makes conclusions on the basis of the observation of results in certain cases (CP 2.622). This general form allows it to be used, for example, to show that what is true in a part (of a population) may be true of the whole population, in which case it is called *quantitative* induction (CP 2.269). Or it may allow us to assign a certain amount of credibility to a hypothesis or proposition based on the fact that its consequences can be experimentally confirmed; in that case it is called *qualitative* induction (CP 2.269).

The Classification of Signs

As mentioned, classification is a different effort than typology; it is an attempt to organize types in a way that shows their affinities. Peirce seems to work with two sorts of classifications in mind; one, for lack of a better name, might be called *hierarchical*, the other *typological*. Peirce's classification of signs is an example of the latter, while his attempt at the classification of the sciences discussed in the first chapter is an example of the former. Indeed, both sorts of classifications were initiated around the same time in his career. In hierarchical classification, which can easily be visualized as a treelike organization, the goal is to show a relation of affinities, dependence or interdependence among the classes with the various levels (cf. CP 1.180). Such a classification, as we saw, has hypernomic divisions: branches, classes, orders, families, etc. (CP 1.230). So, for example, logic was shown to be dependent upon phenomenology, which in turn is dependent on mathematics, etc. Clearly, this sort of classification is modeled after natural classifications, such as those found in botany and zoology. It generally is developed in a posteriori fashion—observation of a large number of specimens suggests the division and characteristics of the class (CP 1.224).

Typological classification, on the other hand, is structured more formally. The classification is based on the formal conditions of the *type* of phenomena, and its classification is generated a priori from the type, "from a connection between the things and a system of formal ideas" (CP 1.223). Mathematical classification is the paradigm here. Thus, in order for something to count as a regular convex polygon (as a mathematical type), it must have certain formal conditions: it must be n-sided, where n is greater than 4, its angles and sides must be equal in number, the sum of its exterior angles must equal 360°, and the sum of its interior angles equals (2n-4)90° (cf. Peirce's example at CP 1.223). Filling in the particulars of the formal conditions will generate a number of classes: pentagon, hexagon, octagon, chilion, etc. Unlike hierarchical classification, the various classes of polygons are not dependent on one another but rather are serially ordered, in the sense that they all satisfy the same formal conditions but in various ways. This seems to be the model for sign classification as well. Indeed, Peirce suggests that classes within logic (hence semeiotic) are generated in the same way (CP 1.223). Each class of sign (using the interim typology) must satisfy at least three of the formal conditions of a sign: that it represent an object, that it represent that object in some respect, and that it create an interpretant that establishes it as a representation of that object; but each class of sign will satisfy those conditions differently. Thus a rhematic iconic legisign will satisfy those conditions differently than a dicent indexical sinsign. The difference, of course, with the mathematical model is that the generation of signs is finite, since the variables concerning the sign are finite in number (as opposed to quantities which are infinite).

This classification is ordered by certain leading principles. First, since a sign in order to be a sign must retain a triadic relation among sign, object, and interpretant, that is, its presentative, representative, and interpretative character, then every sign in the classification will exhibit one of the divisions within each of the three trichotomies,[37] for example, in terms of its presentative aspect, a sign may signify primarily through the quality it has (i.e., as a qualisign), represent its object iconically, and allow for interpretations that are primarily rhematic. This might be called the *composition rule*.

Second, keeping in mind that phenomenology is a more foundational formal science than semeiotic, the classification of the signs is determined by certain leading principles derived from phenomenology and the study of the categories (CP 2.233). The most general of these is that a possible or a "first" (including qualities, feelings, etc.) can determine nothing but a first and a necessitant or "third" (including habits, conventions, laws, etc.) can only determine nothing but a necessitant (LW 84; cf. CP 2.235–2.236).[38] According to Peirce, qualisigns, icons, and rhemes are phenomenologically typed as firsts (of thirds) or possibles, while legisigns, symbols, and arguments are phenomenologically typed as thirds (of thirds). Consequently, given the three trichotomies of signs and the composition rule, the total possible permutation of twenty-seven classes is reduced to ten.[39] This might be called the *qualification rule*.[40] This can be more succinctly stated in the following way: the presentative aspect of a sign can only be combined with representative aspects which are equal to or lower than the presentative's phenomenological type; the representative aspect of the sign can only be combined with inter-pretative aspects which are equal to or lower than the representative's phenomenological type. This, formally speaking, produces the following ten *classes*[41] of signs (CP 2.254–263), whose character will be fleshed out a bit later:

1. rhematic iconic qualisigns
2. rhematic iconic sinsigns
3. rhematic indexical sinsigns
4. dicentic indexical sinsigns
5. rhematic iconic legisigns
6. rhematic indexical legisigns
7. dicentic indexical legisigns
8. rhematic symbolic legisigns
9. dicentic symbolic legisigns
10. argumentive symbolic legisigns

The following corollaries result from this rule:

a. Qualisigns will always represent their objects iconically.
b. Qualisigns will always be interpreted rhematically.
c. Icons will always be interpreted rhematically.
d. Arguments can only represent their objects symbolically.

Third, although every sign requires an element from each of the three trichotomies, some subset of these will predominate over the others; for example, the fact that a sign is a qualisign may be more significant than the fact that it is also a rhematic icon (cf. CP 2.264). This might be called the *dominance rule*.[42] A corollary to this rule is the realization that in ordinary discussion of the sign, one of the three aspects may come to represent the entire sign. For example, Peirce argues that the most fundamental trichotomy of signs is the division into icon, index, and symbol (CP 2.275), and often many use these aspects to represent the entire sign.

Fourth, there is what might be called the *instantiation rule*. This is the claim that all signs in order to count as such must be instantiated, therefore expressed in some sinsign. A qualisign cannot actually act as a sign until it is embodied (CP 2.244); nor can the legisign, which can only signify through an instance of its application (CP 2.246), the latter being called a *replica* (CP 2.246); and a replica is a sinsign (CP 2.246). This should not be confused with the claim that a sign signifies primarily by means of being a sinsign. In the last case, it is the fact that it has temporal and spatial uniqueness that gives it the capability to represent something. But the fact that something occupies space and time may not be as significant as the fact that it has a certain quality which serves as the basis for its representative capacity; however, anything which does so signify must be embodied or instantiated. Thus a qualisign must be instantiated in a sinsign, but its basis of representation is its quality rather than its spatial-temporal uniqueness.

Fifth, what might be called the *inclusion rule* expresses the following idea: within the same aspect of the sign, the division with the higher phenomenological status involves the division(s) with lower ones. Thus a sinsign always involves a qualisign (CP 2.245); a legisign always involves a sinsign (and so indirectly a qualisign) (CP 2.246). Indices involve icons (CP 2.248); symbols involve indices (and so indirectly icons) (CP 2.249, 2.293. 2.295). Dicents involve rhemes (CP 2.251); arguments involve dicents (and so indirectly rhemes) (CP 2.253). In other words, the inclusion rule suggests that there is no such thing as a pure symbol, for example, since it will always include an index and icon. It may be the case that the included sign serves as the vehicle by which the principal sign conveys information or refers to its object (cf. CP 2.257 and 2.260 for examples). The fact that a symbol includes an index allows it to refer, and the fact that it includes an icon allows it to signify (CP 2.293). A corollary that follows from the inclusion rule is that in the list of ten classes of signs given above, the higher numbered signs include, either directly or indirectly, all the lesser numbered signs.[43]

The rules of inclusion and instantiation allow for several subclasses of signs (CP 2.265). There is a difference between a sinsign which acts purely as a sinsign, in the sense that it serves as a basis of the representation of its object, and a sinsign that is simply the replica of a legisign (CP 2.265). The same is true, according to Peirce, in the case of indices and dicisigns, when they serve, respectively, as replicas of symbols and arguments (CP 2.265). Other subclasses of signs are created when the normal varieties of qualisigns, icons, and rhemes are involved or included *directly* in sinsigns, indices, and dicisigns, respectively, and *indirectly* in legisigns, symbols, and arguments, respectively (CP 2.265). For example, an ordinary proposition is classified according to Peirce as a dicentic symbolic legisign (CP 2.262), but when a proposition serves as a premise in an argument, then the dicentic symbolic legisign has acquired "a new force," according to Peirce (CP 2.265). Its inclusion in an argument (as opposed to being a simple assertion of fact) gives it a different character which demands that it be called a sort of subclass of this class of sign.

Before attempting to give some character to the ten classes of signs, it's important to keep in mind two important qualifications to this process. First, in Peirce's own words: "It is a nice problem to say to what class a given sign belongs; since all the circumstances of the case have to be considered. But it is seldom requisite to be very accurate; for if one does not locate the sign precisely, one will easily come near enough to its character for any ordinary purpose of logic" (CP 2.265).

Second, there is a tendency by Peirce to treat these as distinct classes of signs, but if the classification rules listed above are the case, then it follows that it is unlikely that there are any signs which fit purely into any of these classifications. By the rule of inclusion, higher phenomenologically typed signs should include lower ones, while the rule of dominance would suggest that a sign, even if it is predominantly iconic, might contain conventional or symbolic elements. Since, by the rule of instantiation, every sign is instantiated in a sinsign, then, for example, a pure qualisign would be impossible to find.[44] This is perhaps why Peirce's examples of each class are few and not entirely clear. Peirce makes allowance for this by creating subclasses which distinguish, for example, sinsigns which are merely instantiations or replicas, and so are degenerate, from sinsigns which act genuinely as such. But still, since one cannot find a case of a symbol that is not instantiated, it is impossible to give an example of a pure symbol. Consequently, a more reasonable account would be to consider these classes not as distinct types of signs but the manner in which a sign can be abstracted, emphasized, or perspectivized for certain purposes. It might be argued that the ten classes of signs are the product of a certain prescision, which allows us to separate out the features of a sign without thereby destroying the unity of those features as expressed in the sign. Actually, it would be easier to take a sign and analyze it in terms of nine basic types, eliminating those which it does not share, showing in what combination the remaining ones exist, then elaborating their organization on the basis of the principles of inclusion and instantiation. But in any case an outline of the various classes is a worthwhile exercise, if not simply for the sake of achieving some depth in understanding the complexity of sign analysis.

Keeping these two qualifications in mind, the ten classes of signs can be articulated in the following ways.

1. Rhematic iconic **qualisign** (the bold indicates the predominant feature). This sort of sign is any sign which acts through the qualities it has as a sign. What predominates in this sort of sign is its presentative character rather than any other aspect, but the presentative character in terms of its qualities rather than anything else. For all practical purposes it must be instantiated in a rhematic iconic sinsign (CP 2.255). Since it is the lowest type, phenomenologically speaking, it does not involve any other type of sign, but every other type will either directly or indirectly involve it. In its more genuine form it could be thought of as any percept or feeling of a quality where the source or object of that quality is somewhat indeterminate or vague, for example, a nebulous patch of color, seeing a blotch of red in an afterimage, hearing the wind blow through an old house, the musty smell while walking in a forest, the aftertaste from a deliciously exotic meal. The qualisign always presents itself iconically as a map waiting for its terrain. As a result, its interpretation is usually directed toward the sign qua quality rather than any object it (possibly or potentially) represents. Its representative capability, then, is rather vague and indeterminate. In the final typology, Peirce calls signs which represent their (dynamic) object in this manner *abstractives* (CP 8.366). As a rheme it adds some information (the informed depth of the sign) but presents information that is more descriptive than factual. In the final typology, Peirce calls signs which inform by description *descriptives* (CP 8.350). For example, if a patch of red is instantiated in an abstract painting (for example, one of Kandinsky's compositions), it could be considered a rhematic iconic qualisign in this regard. Abstract paintings as a style focus the interpretation of the painting toward the characteristics displayed on the canvas (its depth) rather than any reference or breadth; but inevitably in the interpretation of such paintings the movement is toward completing the interpretation by speculating on its reference (this tonal quality of the

red expresses anger or freedom of movement). In abstract painting the reference has more possibilities, in the sense that many are possible; but whether they are actual is less clear than, let's say, a landscape painting might be. But in any case seeking breadth in the interpretation of an abstract painting always involves iconic representation: the red patch is an image of a feeling (let's say anger or excitement or danger), for example, or the asymmetry of the composition maps a feeling of discord. There is a similar case when a sound is instantiated as a note produced by a musical instrument in the context of a musical piece. The sound taken alone (abstracting away from its instantiation) may be treated as a (rhematic iconic) qualisign. In and of itself it may have a certain tonal quality or timbre which, for a certain interpreter, represents a vague feeling by similarity, a feeling interpreted in its essential and possible outlines, rather than in any definitive or lawlike way.

2. Rhematic **iconic sinsign**. For all practical purposes, a rhematic iconic sinsign is simply an instantiated icon, such as an individual diagram (CP 2.256). However, in its purest or genuine form, it would be any icon which, because of its singularity or individuality, has the power to represent its object as similar to the sign. For example, we might be inclined to think that the only existing sculpture of Socrates is the way Socrates looked, as opposed to the several existing portraits and sculptures of Jesus, all of which represent his face and features differently. Because it is interpreted rhematically, the emphasis is on the features of similarity. Rhematic iconic sinsigns involve qualisigns, since any sinsign has some quality to it. But although the quality may contribute to some degree to the sign's power to represent, still primarily it is its singularity more than anything else which contributes to that power.

3. **Rhematic indexical sinsign**. These are indices which act primarily to indicate an object without conveying much about its sense or depth. In its purest form this is any singular sign which, because of its unique spatial and temporal location, is interpreted as pointing to or drawing attention to its object. For example, a *spontaneous* cry would be a rhematical indexical sinsign (CP 2.256). The cry must be spontaneous and not have any conventional or lawlike associations such as a grunt (from lifting a heavy load) or a scream of pain or terror would have. Because the spontaneous cry is of an indeterminate nature, it is interpreted rhematically, in terms of its essential qualities; what it represents, therefore, is also rather vague. It will involve a qualisign (for example, the intensity, pitch, or loudness of the cry) which can act iconically to represent, potentially, some object; the loudness of the cry might represent the utterer's attempt to get my attention; or the intensity, the utterer's desperation. However,

it's found more often in its practical (or degenerate) form as a replica of a rhematical indexical legisign, that is, precisely as an instance of a cry of pain or terror or as a replica of a demonstrative pronoun which has the purpose of pointing to or drawing attention to a certain object.

4. **Dicentic** indexical **sinsign.** These are indices which not only indicate their object but also are able to present some sense or depth about the object they refer to. It is any sign which is able to provide information about its object by being actually affected by that object. For example, a windvane (CP 2.257), as it is presently being pushed in a certain direction by the wind, would be a case of this sort of sign. Because of the physical connection between the wind and the windvane, an interpreter could ascribe as factual a certain property to the wind (namely, its direction). In the final typology, Peirce later calls a sign in this regard a *designative* (CP 8.350). The emphasis here is on its interpretative aspect, the fact that the sign promotes the sense of a factual and informational revelation about the sign and its object. The object is more determinate and its interpretation more factual for that reason. This type of sign directly involves a rhematic iconic sinsign, specifically in its capacity to convey something about the sense or depth of the object. It involves an icon (sinsign) which, in the case of the windvane, is the manner in which the possible directions of the windvane map out and parallel the possible directions of the wind, and it therefore contributes to the way in which the information is conveyed. In order to do that, it directly involves a rheme (iconic sinsign), that is, the windvane must be already viewed in terms of its essential direction-giving capacity. This type of sign also directly involves a rhematic indexical sinsign, specifically in terms of its capacity to refer to its object. As an index of this sort it draws attention or points to the object to which it refers; and it is interpreted, in that regard, essentially in terms of the referring capacity.

5. Rhematic **iconic legisign.** These are signs which represent likenesses in a predominantly conventional way. A diagram (CP 2.258) or graph, for example, represents its object by showing a similarity between relations that exist on the graph and the relations that exist in its object (the economy, for example). The graph itself, the x-y coordinates, lines, curves, numbers, etc., are legisigns. A topographical map would be another example. It uses a certain relation among conventional symbols to mirror relations that exist among elements in the terrain. The distance between contour lines, marked by numbers, parallels the height and contour of the terrain. Color coding indicates relatively flat versus mountainous terrain. Rivers are lines drawn to match the rivers in the actual terrain, while trails may be indicated by dotted lines. There are no pure iconic legisigns, since legisigns must be instantiated in some sinsign. Thus every instantiation of

an iconic legisign is an iconic sinsign. These sorts of signs are generally interpreted rhematically. So, for example, the sense of the relation between trade balance and interest rates would be paralleled in the sense of the curve on the graph.

6. **Rhematic indexical legisign.** This is any conventional sign which acts primarily as an index. Demonstrative pronouns are paradigm cases (CP 2.259). It is interpreted simply as indicating or pointing to the object to which it refers while conveying a minimum of sense or depth concerning that object. This sign is always instantiated in a rhematical indexical sinsign, so there are no pure cases of such signs.

7. **Dicentic indexical legisign.** This is any conventional sign which not only acts as an index but also simultaneously tells us some information about its object through correlating that conventional sign (usually a name) with what is indicated by the sign. For example, a street cry (CP 2.260) (such as "hot dogs, get your hot dogs") not only indicates but also tells us the content of what is indicated. It involves a rhematic indexical legisign in order to refer to its object (here is something here and now) and conveys any depth by involving a rhematic iconic legisign, i.e., it conveys the depth of that object through using the name of the object (hence its sense in the most general terms). Because these are correlated in the sign, they are interpreted as revealing something factual, and so it is dicentic. Because it is always instantiated in a dicent sinsign, there are no pure cases of this sort of sign.

8. **Rhematic symbolic** legisign. This is any conventional sign which correlates with its object primarily through some conventional, habitual, or lawlike means, and acts primarily in conveying a general sense or depth about the object it represents. The paradigm is the common noun (CP 2.260). The word "dog" is first of all a legisign, which signifies or represents general features about dogs (a dog has four legs, barks, etc.), and so it is interpreted rhematically. The word "dog" conveys the depth of the object without really establishing that the depth is about some particular dog or class of dogs. It is always instantiated in a rhematic indexical sinsign, so there are no pure examples of this type. The instance or replica is always indexical since the appearance of the individual replica acts to "cause" the association between the legisign and object to be established on each occasion.

9. **Dicentic symbolic** legisign. This is any conventional sign which establishes a correlation with its object and so provides some information about it. As such it is usually interpreted as conveying something factual, hence its dicentic characteristic. The paradigm example is that of a proposition (CP 2.261) ("This is a big dog"), which, in its essence,

establishes a correlation between the subject (the object named) and the predicate, the object in regard to its depth. It involves a rhematic symbol in order to convey the sense or depth of the object and a rhematic indexical legisign to indicate the subject of that information. It is instantiated in a dicent sinsign.

10. **Argumentive** symbolic legisign. This is any conventional sign which reveals the lawlike or habitual characteristics of its object. The paradigm case is that of an inference of an argument, which shows the connection between one set of propositions (the premises) and another (the conclusion). It is instantiated or replicated in a dicent sinsign.

3 Critical Logic

Critical logic is concerned with those types of signs, such as legisigns, symbols, dicents, and arguments, that are capable of expressing and inferring information. It is specifically concerned with these in regard to the accuracy and truth of the information they convey, since that is critical for determining the final interpretants of signs. Critical logic, then, is designed to discern "the formal conditions of the truth of symbols" (CP 1.559, 2.93, 4.116). Put succinctly, though nominally, the primary formal condition for truth is that the symbol correspond with its object (CP 2.541, 5.553, 5.554, 6.350). This is a very traditional conception of truth, but Peirce's account of "correspondence" expands this idea in an original way. First, truth belongs exclusively to a certain kind of symbol, the proposition (CP 5.553) (the dicent symbol). As discussed earlier, every proposition contains a subject (or set of subjects) and a predicate (CP 5.553, 2.472). "The subject is a sign; the predicate is a sign; and the proposition is a sign that the predicate is a sign of that of which the subject is a sign" (CP 5.553). So truth concerns the correspondence between the (propositional) symbol and its object. But the sense of "correspondence" in this case is better understood under the idea of what has come to be called *convergence* (CP 7.110):[1] " . . . there is a general *drift* in the history of human thought which will lead it to one general agreement, one catholic consent" (CP 8.12). This can be articulated in the following way. Since thought is of the nature of a sign (CP 5.553) and a proposition is both a product and a process of thinking, "in that case, then, if we can find out the right method of thinking and can follow it out—the right method of transforming signs—then truth can be nothing more nor less than the last result to which the following out of this method would ultimately carry us" (CP 5.553). Truth then is not simply the correspondence of a (propositional) symbol with its object but the correspondence of an object represented in the final and valid inferential display of that original proposition, the manner in which the inferential consequences of a proposition, or the arguments related to that proposition, converge toward a certain outcome. In other words, as expressed in the principle behind the pragmatic maxim,[2] the truth of a proposition lies where its inferential consequences lead. As Peirce describes it, "truth is that concordance of an abstract statement with the ideal limit towards which endless investigation would tend to bring scientific belief . . . " (CP 5.565). Consequently, the formal condition of truth, the subject matter of critical logic, leads exactly to the question of the right method of thinking, that is, the question of valid inferencing or arguments: "we may say that the purpose of signs—which is the purpose of thought—is to bring truth to expression. The law under which a sign must be true is the law of inference; and the signs of a scientific intelligence must, above all other conditions, be such as to lend themselves to inference. Hence, the illative relation is the primary and paramount semiotic relation" (CP 2.444n1).

Critical logic aims to discern the right method of reasoning, understood primarily as inference: "it classifies reasonings and determines their value" (MS 452: 9). Inference can expand and develop signs by incorporating new information about already systematized signs, or it can increase the connectedness among those systematized signs. There are then two basic types of inference, synthetic or ampliative, a process of discovery which increases the amount of information in the system of signs, and analytic or explicative, which involves inferences that show the connection among information already discovered (CP 2.623). Inferences of discovery include abduction and induction, while deduction is the primary analytic form of inference (CP 2.623); all other types of inference, including analogy, are some combination or attenuation of these basic types (CP 5.274).

The Basis of Critical Logic

Critical logic is concerned with valid inferences, that is, good reasoning. The question is how such validity is established. In one sense it is answered by showing how critical logic is grounded in the disciplines which precede it hierarchically in Peirce's classification of the sciences, as they were outlined in chapter 1.

Logic is dependent upon the findings from the disciplines of mathematics, phenomenology, ethics, and aesthetics—and in a certain regard there is a division of labor in this. On the one hand, since mathematics is the science of necessary reasoning and inference is a form of reasoning, then critical logic must look to mathematics for guidance in this regard. On the other, since critical logic is concerned with reasoning in the context of *experience*, it must rely to a certain extent on the findings in phenomenology, which studies the general structure of experience. This was certainly true for semeiotic grammar, especially in regard to the analysis and classification of signs. But in addition, and to the extent that critical logic is concerned with *good* reasoning, it must rely on ethics, which in turn is dependent upon aesthetics. Since the last two disciplines were not fully developed in Peirce, except for some general pronouncements, he does not make the connection between ethics and logic specific. However, the connection between mathematics and critical logic is a bit more elaborated.

As Peirce argues, mathematics is the science of necessary reasoning (CP 4.229).[3] Put differently, mathematics is concerned with necessary reasoning per se, regardless of whether its hypotheses correspond to anything in nature or not (cf. NEM 4: 194; CP 4.233, 4.240, 1.184, 1.240). This is distinct from critical logic which, as Peirce suggests, is "a science of truth" (CP 1.247); it is concerned with the *truth of propositions* (CP 2.778). Mathematics, on the other hand, is "only a science of the consequences of hypotheses" (CP 1.247). Thus logical deduction is concerned with the necessary connection among propositions supposed to be *true*, as opposed to simply being supposed. However, since critical logic is concerned in part with *necessary* reasoning, it is dependent upon the character of mathematics (CP 4.240). In fact, Peirce claims that a certain sort of mathematics, *formal* logic (sometimes called *exact* [CP 3.616] or *symbolic* [CP 4.372])—which is nothing but mathematics applied to logic (CP 4.263)—can provide the systematic grounding of the validity of the arguments critical logic supposes are valid. More specifically, Peirce suggests this role for his algebra of logic and the logic of relations (which, in turn, serve as a fundamental inspiration for his phenomenology).

Formal logic is the application of mathematical reasoning to the discernment of valid versus invalid reasoning (CP 2.192); strictly speaking, then, it is a part of mathematics (CP 1.283, 4.240). Thus Peirce's work in the logic of relations is more an example of mathematical logic than of critical logic.[4] "The great difference between the logic of relatives and ordinary logic is that the former regards the form of relation in all its generality and in its different possible species while the latter is tied down to the matter of the single relation of similarity" (CP 4.5). The purpose of formal logic is not to aid in the drawing of inferences (CP 4.373) but to further the investigation of the theory of logic, "to help the study of logical principles" (CP 3.485). But for this very reason "deductive logic can really not be understood without the study of the logic of relatives" (CP 3.641). The logic of relatives is able to provide a proof for the basic sort of inferences found in critical logic. Peirce shows in his logic of relations that the relation of inclusion (CP 3.47) is the most fundamental logical relation. Inclusion can be understood simply as a logical part-whole relation, so that it defines the idea that a part is included in a whole. Primitive relations such as equality can, then, be defined in terms of inclusion, so that i and j are identical if everything that can be said of i can be said of j and conversely (CP 3.398); "all equality is inclusion in, but the converse is not true; hence inclusion is a wider concept than equality" (CP 3.47n1). Similarly, with the most primitive logical relation of implication. The implication of p—>q means that every r which includes p is an r which includes q (CP 3.165). Since implication is the essence of any inference, "it can be mathematically proved that every possible necessary inference from two premises, both having the same form as the conclusion, must depend upon a relation of *inclusion*" (CP 2.558); more generally,

> To say that an inference is correct is to say that if the premises are true the conclusion is also true; or that every possible state of things in which the premises should be true would be included among the possible state of things in which the conclusion would be true. We are thus led to the copula of inclusion. (CP 2.710)

Every argument involves an inference; every inference in its general form involves an implication—if p, then q; every implication is dependent upon inclusion, which in turn is established as fundamental in the logic of relations.

From this point, the three basic sorts of inferences—-deduction, induction, and abduction—can be derived. Stated in general terms, Peirce notes that the main characteristic of the relation of inclusion is that it is transitive (CP 2.710, 3.47), that is, "that what is included in something included in anything is itself included in that thing; or, that if A is B and B is C, then A is C" (CP 2.710). This is the classic syllogism known as *Barbara*, or hypothetical syllogism, as it is currently called. All other deductive syllogisms can be derived from Barbara (CP 2.620). Moreover, the syllogisms pertaining to induction and abduction can be derived from (statistical) deduction so understood (CP 2.715, 2.619 ff.).

The Anatomy of Arguments

Peirce sees the analysis of the constituent parts of arguments and their classification as part of the job of critical logic (CP 2.205). We have seen that inclusion is the fundamental relation of any inference, and an inference is the essential quality of any argument. Any argument can be analyzed into the following parts:[5] the leading principle, the premises, the colligation, involvement, and the conclusion.

A premise is a proposition which contributes to the determination of a conclusion (CP 2.582). Thus a premise is not simply a proposition but is implicitly understood to be colligated with another premise in order to infer the conclusion. The conclusion is also a proposition, but it is the determination of the premises, their upshot. The conclusion of an argument is its interpretant, understood as the *product* of the sign process (CP 2.253, 2.95). Colligation is simply the operation which consists in bringing the different premises together and applying them, the one to the other (CP 2.553). To claim that

> All humans are mortal
> All citizens of the U.S. are human
> Therefore, all citizens of the U.S. are mortal

is really to argue that "All humans are mortal and all citizens of the U.S. are human." Involvement is the idea of the transference of the facts from the premises to the conclusion (CP 2.553).

But by and large the most important aspect of the argument is its leading principle. Peirce defines *leading principle* (or guiding principle) as essentially a habit of thought controlling and validating inference from premise to conclusion (CP 2.462–465, 2.588, 3.160–168, 4.69). In other words, the leading principle is the essence or expression of inference. In this regard it could be understood as the argument's final interpretant (cf. CP 2.462, 2.465, 2.576, 2.588). So determining the validity of an argument hinges on determining the truth of a leading principle (CP 2.463). In turn, if one can guarantee the validity of a leading principle, then, given true premises, the conclusion will have a guarantee of being either necessarily or probably true, depending on the type of argument (CP 2.464).

The term "leading principle," however, has a somewhat ambiguous meaning. In one sense it means the particular rule of inference which guides a class of arguments (CP 3.164); so, for example, what Peirce calls the *nota notae*, or what is often called the transitive relation, the classic syllogistic form of Barbara, is the leading principle of all deductive syllogism (CP 2.474, 2.590, 4.76). But, in another sense, a leading principle means the guiding principle for an entire form of reasoning, so that there would be a leading principle each for deduction, induction, and abduction (CP 4.74).

Deduction

Put simply, logical deduction is an argument which shows a *necessary* connection between premises and the conclusion, so that *if* the premises *were* true, the conclusion would be, too (CP 2.778). Consequently, logical deduction is a form of necessary reasoning (CP 2.267), and, of course, mathematics is the science of necessary reasoning (CP 4.229). Logical deduction then must find its basis in mathematical reasoning.

Necessary reasoning involves the study of diagrams in a broad sense. Diagrams are icons in the sense that the relation among the elements in the diagram is isomorphic to its object; examples would be a drawing of an isosceles triangle, the standard symbolic form of an argument, or an algebraic equation (NEM 3: 869). Peirce makes the rather novel claim[6] that necessary reasoning is a sort of experimental procedure (CP 3.560), but one that involves constructs (i.e., diagrams) rather than naturally existing events. Peirce claims:

> By diagrammatic reasoning, I mean reasoning which constructs a diagram according to a precept expressed in general terms, performs experiments upon this diagram, notes their results, assures itself that similar experiments performed upon any diagram constructed according to the same precept would have the same results, and expresses this in general terms. (NEM 4: 47–48)

This procedure is outlined by Peirce somewhat as follows (cf. NEM 3: 749):

1.   The statement of the hypothesis in general terms.
2.   The construction of a diagram which is an icon of that hypothesis.

3.   Observation of the diagram.
4.   The determination that the relation observed would be found
        in every iconic representation of the hypothesis.
5.   Statement of the results in general terms.

Necessary reasoning, understood as diagrammatic reasoning, has two species, which are distinguished by the process of observation in (3) above. A *corollarial* deduction is one which represents the conditions of the conclusion in the diagram and, from observation of this diagram, determines the truth of the conclusion (CP 2.267, NEM 3: 869, CP 4.234). That is to say, the conclusion is immediately present in the diagram. For example, the conclusion of an argument such as

> All humans are mammals
> All mammals are vertebrates
> Therefore, all humans are vertebrates

is immediately transparent in its Venn diagram (see figure 5).

On the other hand, *theorematic* reasoning is one which, having represented the conditions of the conclusion in a diagram, performs an ingenious experiment upon the diagram and, by the observation of the diagram so modified, ascertains the truth of the conclusion (CP 2.267, 4.234). In this case, the conditions for the conclusion are represented in the diagram, but the diagram is not sufficient to yield the conclusion in an immediate way. Experimentation with the diagram, however, will yield such a result.[7] An example of this is found in ordinary Euclidean geometry (NEM 3: 896). One first states the hypothesis: *if* two lines are parallel to the same line, then they are parallel to one another; the second step is to construct a diagram in which two lines are parallel to the same line. At this point the conclusion

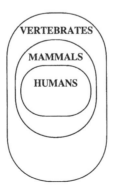

Figure 5. Venn diagram as an illustration of corollarial reasoning.

is not transparent. However, if one draws a transversal through the three lines, then because the first two lines are parallel to one another, it follows that their alternate interior angles are equal. One continues experiments with strategies for deriving the conclusion until that conclusion is reached in an orderly fashion. In this process one must bring into the matter other theorems in order to bring out what is implicit or mediate in the diagram.

The procedure in step (4) above seems to be what Peirce refers to as the "test of inconceivability" (CP 2.29), used to ascertain whether or not there is a necessary connection. This consists in trying to determine whether or not its denial is inconceivable (CP 2.29, 3.387). However, Peirce emphasizes that "inconceivable" should not mean merely unrealizable in imagination today but unrealizable after indefinite training and education: "It certainly must be admitted by every reasonable disputant, that every proposition whose denial is in that sense absolutely and eternally inconceivable is [true]" (CP 2.29). In other words, the necessity of necessary inferences is, like any other claim, subject to fallibility, and the truth of its necessity is established in the long run. As an example Peirce mentions the Euclidean axiom "The whole is greater than any of its parts." Its denial seems inconceivable and seemed so for a couple of thousand years. Yet Cantor's transfinite mathematics could prove a counterexample. The set of even natural numbers is a subset of the natural numbers, yet both collections are infinite; consequently a part is quantitatively equal to the whole.

As a whole the procedure outlined for necessary reasoning also nicely illustrates the semeiotic process: the object (a hypothesis) is represented in a sign (the diagram), which then determines a certain interpretation of it (its interpretant), that is, follows out the consequences of its diagram (cf. CP 1.240). Deduction can be thought of as an inference which allows us to expand or complicate the system just on the basis of the information that is already contained in the system. It doesn't discover new information so much as make explicit what information is already implicit in the system but not directly expressed. We may know that all human beings are mortal and that Enoch is a human being, but it may not be explicitly known that Enoch is mortal, although now that can be established. So, technically speaking, as Peirce suggests, there is really no change of information that occurs (CP 2.423).

Deductions are also concerned with probable relations (CP 2.267). Deductions of probability, on the other hand, are deductions whose interpretants represent them to be concerned with ratios of frequency (CP 2. 268). They are either *statistical deductions* or *probable deductions proper* (CP 2.268).[8] A statistical deduction is a deduction whose interpretant represents it to reason concerning ratios of frequency, but to reason concerning them with absolute certainty (CP 2.268). As mentioned, Peirce argues that a formal form of induction and abduction can be derived from statistical deduction. A probable deduction proper is a deduction whose interpretant does not represent that its conclusion is certain but that precisely analogous reasonings would produce true conclusions from true premises in the majority of cases, in the long run of experience (CP 2.268). Peirce gives the following example of the latter (CP 2.694):

> About two percent of persons wounded in the liver recover.
> This man has been wounded in the liver.
> Therefore, there are two chances out of a hundred that he will recover.

This has the general form of deduction: rule, case, result. But unlike deduction proper, the rule here is probable, that is, not that every member of a class will have such and such features, but a certain percentage (CP 2.696), that is to say, the difference between saying that "every M is a P" and "the proportion p of the M's are P's" (CP 2.695).

Peirce gives the following example of statistical deduction (CP 2.701):

> A little more than half of all human births are males.
> Hence, probably a little over half of all the births in New York during any one year are males.

If the implicit premise is supplied in this case—"There were x number of births in New York this year"—then, again, the argument is the typical deductive form of rule, case, and result. However, the difference is in the case which is a "numerous set" taken at random from the M's—so the difference is in the case rather than the rule.

The System of Existential Graphs as a Representation of Natural Deduction

The system of existential graphs was meant as a means of expressing "natural" deduction (a deductive logic which assumes a number of inference types) in a clear and obvious way: it makes "literally visible before one's very eyes the operation of thinking *in actu*" (CP 4.6). Peirce believed that practice with existential graphs would enable one "to use the graphs to work out difficult inferences with expedition" (CP 4.617); consequently, it was meant simply as an educational tool (CP 4.619), and Peirce believed that it should be taught "to boys and girls before grammar" (CP 4.619). The existential graphs were never intended as propositional

Figure 6. An example of a cut.

calculus but simply as devices for logical analysis.[9] The true work of grounding a deductive system was to be found in the logic of relations.

The system of existential graphs was divided into four parts: alpha, beta, gamma, and delta. Alpha was the most developed and concerned the logic of propositions (CP 4.394–402, 4.414); beta was somewhat developed and concerned the logic of quantification (CP 4.403–408, 4.416); the gamma part, which was to deal with logical relations in general, was never completed (CP 4.409–4.413, 4.573–584); while the delta part—which was to deal with modalities—was never started (cf. MS 500).

To illustrate the sense of the system, we might consider some of the elementary representations, while referring the reader to scholars who have pursued this in some detail.[10] Alpha is based on the operators of conjunction and negation. Peirce's symbol for negation is called a *cut*, which is a finely drawn line which encircles the expression that is to be negated (see figure 6). The interior of the cut is called its *area*, and a cut together with its area is called an *enclosure*. On the basis of these definitions, the fundamental types of propositions—negation, conjunction, disjunction, and implication—can be graphed (see figure 7).

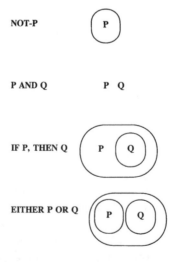

Figure 7. The basic types of connectives expressed as existential graphs.

Figure 8.

Then, on the basis of certain rules, one shows how it is possible to transform one proposition into another. For example, given the proposition shown in figure 8, one may be permitted the proposition shown in figure 9 (by means of the rule of "addition").

Induction

Whereas deduction shows the result of applying a rule to a certain case, induction draws a rule from the results of a sample of cases. "Induction is where we generalize from a number of cases of which something is true, and infer that the same thing is true of a whole class ... " (CP 2.624). "By induction, we conclude that facts, similar to observed facts, are true in cases not examined" (CP 2.636). Whereas deduction involves the inference of a result from a case under a rule, induction concludes a rule from the observation of a result in a certain case (CP 2.622).

There are three types of induction, according to Peirce. The first is *crude* induction. It is the weakest kind. It consists in denying that a general kind of event ever will occur on the ground that it never has or seldom has occurred. Thus it would be strange to be afraid that one's house will be struck by lightning while one is on a visit to another town (cf. CP 2.257n1). Clearly, without such inductions, we could not get along in life (cf. CP 2.257; also CP 2.257n1).

Quantitative induction is the second type. If we want to determine whether an individual member of a class, P, has some character Q, this is accomplished by taking a fair sample of the Ps; an estimate of the proportion of that sample which has Q then suggests that the entire class of P has that same proportion (CP 2.758). In other words, quantitative

Figure 9.

induction involves an argument from a random sample (CP 2.269). Two conditions must be observed in order to ensure success in the method of random sampling. First, the sample must be a genuinely random one (CP 2.725 ff., 1.95). There must be no bias or preconception involved, so that the choice is completely arbitrary. Second, the character, Q (for P), must be chosen in advance of the examination of the sample, that is, it must satisfy the condition of predesignation (CP 2.735 ff., 2.790). If the second condition is violated and induction is used to discover a characteristic of P, then the results are not warranted or guaranteed. To illustrate this last point, Peirce selects a sample of names and ages of the first five poets mentioned in Wheeler's *Biographical Dictionary*; in comparing the age of death, he discovers that in each case the difference between the two digits, divided by three, leaves a remainder of one; the first digit raised to the power of the second and divided by three leaves a remainder of one. Yet there is not the slightest reason to believe that the next poet's age of death would possess those characters (CP 2.738).

The third type of induction is called *qualitative* (CP 2.269); it is of more general utility than the others (CP 2.759). This is the sort of induction that is involved in the verification or confirmation of a hypothesis:[11] "A verification of a general prediction is a method which consists in finding or making the conditions of the prediction and in concluding that it will be verified about as often as it is experimentally found to be verified" (CP 2.269; cf. CP 7.89). A hypothesis can be formulated as a set of predictions; consequently, in proportion as those predictions occur, the hypothesis receives a corresponding verification. As Peirce explains this in more detail, it is the final part of the process of the verification of a scientific hypothesis. After an investigator has formulated a hypothesis by abduction and deduced the testable consequence of that hypothesis, he proceeds to test those consequences (CP 2.759, 7.220). Based on that evidence he combines it to make an evaluation as to whether the hypothesis has been proved, is well on its way to being proved, is unworthy of further attention, or ought to be modified and whether the results can suggest a better hypothesis (CP 2.759).

Abduction

Peirce's notion of abduction (variously called *retroduction* [NEM 4: 344] and *hypothesis* [CP 8.227]) is his most original contribution to the logic of inference, although he credits Aristotle with its original formulation (CP 7.249). His view of abduction also undergoes evolution.

In his earlier analyses, although abduction has a different logical form than induction, it still performs the same function as induction, that is, providing evidence for a hypothesis. His later view suggests that abduction has a function completely different from providing evidence for hypotheses, namely, the formation of hypotheses.[12]

In Kepler's time, the dominant theory suggested that the planets orbited the earth in a circular fashion. This was not changed by the adoption of the heliocentric hypothesis, proposed by Copernicus and then adopted by Galileo. The difficulty that Kepler encountered was that the observations of the positions of the planets (for example of Mars), as charted by the observations of Tyco Brahe, were anomalous with the circular orbit hypothesis. Finally, after many false steps, he took the bold one of proposing a new hypothesis, that the planets orbited in an ellipse about the sun rather than a circle, and by doing so he accommodated what the observations suggested (cf. CP 2.97).

Consider the case of the continental drift theory in geology. In the early part of the twentieth century, the dominant theory concerning the formation of the earth was the so-called contractionist one, which described the earth as having originated as a much hotter body that has since cooled and contracted. Thus the continents were formed as they are, as a direct result of this cooling process. There was vertical motion as the planet cooled but very little horizontal motion, so the oceans and the continents should not have changed their positions relative to one another.

But the striking fit of the eastern South American and western African coastlines would suggest that there was some continental drift, that the continents were connected at one point in time. This is precisely the "surprising or anomalous" event which influenced Alfred Wegener's hypothesis, developed between 1910 and 1915 "under the direct impression produced by the coastlines on either side of the Atlantic."[13] Of course, it wasn't until much later that it was accepted by the majority of geologists, and only after additional theories were proposed which could provide a reasonable account of the mechanism for continental drift.

Abduction is not a process by which we confirm hypotheses; it is only the process by which we arrive at plausible accounts of surprising events. It seeks to develop new hypotheses for testing by discovering ones that are likely to account for events not accountable by means of existing ones.

Abduction begins with a certain anomaly, an anomaly that is generated when certain observed phenomena do not fit into a standard or received pattern of reasoning or hypothesis. Extrapolating a bit, Peirce argues that abduction has the following reasoning pattern:

There is some surprising or anomalous observation or event, E_1 [it is surprising or anomalous from the viewpoint of a certain received or well-understood hypothesis, H_1, concerning it].
This event would not be surprising under another hypothesis, H_2 [i.e., E would follow from H_2].
Therefore, there is some justification in believing H_2 to be the case, i.e., H_2 is plausible [since it accounts for E]. (Cf. CP 5.189)

Abduction is not concerned with determining the truth of a hypothesis but its *plausibility*, based primarily on the ability of the hypothesis to explain (cf. CP 2.662, 7.223). The plausibility of a hypothesis is constituted, at least, by the fact that the anomaly which prompted the hypothesis would be resolved (CP 2.662). There are other factors as well: the proposed hypothesis must be, in principle, testable; it must be likely and have a certain naturalness; and there must be the consideration of the economy in the testing (CP 7.220, 7.223).

Consider the case of Ignaz Semmelweis, an example which Carl Hempel uses often.[14] Semmelweis, a practicing physician at the Vienna General Hospital from 1844 to 1848, was in charge of the obstetrics ward when a very puzzling and tragic set of circumstances arose. An outbreak of puerperal or "childbed" fever occurred in both divisions of the ward, but the first division had a much higher rate than the second division. Several hypotheses were proposed. One was that the phenomenon was due to certain "telluric-atmospheric conditions," in other words, something in the air. But this particular hypothesis would not survive the plausibility test of abduction because, as Semmelweis reasoned, it would not account for the anomaly, namely, the difference in the incidence of puerperal fever in the two divisions. Because patients in the two divisions were presumably breathing the same air, if there were something in the air causing their condition, they should all be affected at approximately the same rate. The abductive logic allowed Semmelweis to dismiss this hypothesis out-of-hand. This was additionally supported by the fact that the incidence of puerperal fever among so-called street births—women who delivered in the open on their way to the hospital—was nonexistent.

Other factors besides plausibility may enter into the question of whether to test a proposed hypothesis. Another consideration might be its *likeliness* (CP 2.663), not to be confused with the credibility achieved by its inductive testing. This might be defined as the sense that in addition to being plausible, the hypothesis stands a good chance of being true, or that it does not involve events or circumstances that would have a low probability of occurring (cf. CP 2.662), therefore, worthy for consideration. For example, in Semmelweis's case it was suggested that the difference in incidence of puerperal fever was due to the fact that the priest and his entourage had to walk past many more beds in the first division on their way to the "sick" room (the room where the dying were given their last rites) than in the second division. The sight of the priest giving the last rites to yet another victim of puerperal fever caused a psychological trauma which, in turn, caused the women to come down with puerperal fever. Now, if this were true, it would account for the difference of incidence of puerperal fever between the first and second division; however, it seems like an unlikely hypothesis. But testing the hypothesis involved little effort or expense; Semmelweis could easily alter the priest's route and observe the results (which, of course, made no difference in the incidence of puerperal fever).

Consider another example. Five months after the British archaeologist Lord Carnarvon uncovered the tomb of King Tutankhamen in the Upper Valley of the Nile, he died under rather mysterious circumstances. Sir Arthur Conan Doyle insisted that his death was due to a "pharaoh's curse." A journalist claimed to have found an ancient hieroglyphic inscription at the entrance to the tomb threatening death to anyone who violated the Pharaoh's resting place. Eventually, twenty-five others associated with the find also died under mysterious circumstances. A recent investigator, Dr. Nicola Di Paolo, head of the department of kidney diseases at a Siena hospital, believes that Carnarvon probably was killed by a hitherto unidentified toxic fungus.[15] His hypothesis was based on an abduction made from a peculiar case he encountered in his clinical experience. A patient of his, a farmer's wife from Siena, felt dizzy and found it difficult to breathe after spending more than eight hours sieving wheat that had gone moldy after being stored for several years in an old barn. Di Paolo carried out an experiment with guinea pigs and rabbits, putting them in a cage with the wheat for eight hours. Several of the animals died and most showed damage to the kidneys and liver. The mold on the wheat seemed to be the culprit. Having been fascinated with the pharaohs and pyramids from an early age and being familiar with the tradition of the curse, Di Paolo reasoned that this sort of toxic mold could easily accumulate in tombs which were closed for centuries. Air and damp could penetrate minute fissures in the walls, permitting the growth of this sort of mold. Thus for Di Paolo, exposure to the mold is the more *likely* explanation for the circumstances under which Carnarvon and the others died.

Why would this hypothesis be preferred to Doyle's "mummy's curse"? The suggestion would be that not only is the hypothesis capable of accounting for the anomaly; the account itself also fits into a type that is considered to belong to an acceptable explanatory framework. Such a framework would be one that draws on certain metaphysical or ontological assumptions that have worked well and continue to do so. Science typically draws on a naturalistic metaphysics, one that assumes the cosmos to be ontologically populated by physical forces, laws, regularities, and observable, measurable entities rather than magic, demons, and occult powers. The justification for relying on such a metaphysics might be rather pragmatic, in the sense that drawing on these types of metaphysically grounded hypotheses results more consistently in the virtues of science: prediction and testability.

Such a metaphysical framework in turn would ground a number of theories; thus hypotheses might be drawn from likely theories. Should it be the case that such hypotheses do not prove credible by testing, then the anomaly can only be resolved by drawing on hypotheses from another theory, thus creating a paradigm shift or revolution. It could also be the case that the metaphysical framework could prove inadequate, in which case the very idea of science might change.

Other Forms of Reasoning

According to Peirce, abduction, deduction, and induction are the principal forms of reasoning; all other types, including analogy, are some combination of these (CP 2.513, 5.277). *Analogy* (that is, analogical reasoning, as opposed to the sense of analogy as illustration or example, which typically employs metaphor) is defined by Peirce as inference that a small collection of objects that agree in various respects may very likely agree in another respect (CP 1.69). For example, we know that of the major planets, Earth, Mars, Jupiter, and Saturn revolve on their axes, and we conclude that the others probably do the same (CP 2.733). The general form of the argument looks something like this:

> S_1, S_2, S_3 are a random sample from a class of things, X, which exhibit certain properties, P_1, P_2, P_3.
> Q also has those properties, P_1, P_2, P_3.
> But the Ss also have the property R.
> Therefore Q probably has the property R, too.

According to Peirce, this sort of inference involves a sequence of induction, abduction, and deduction. First, since the Ss are samples of Xs and Ss also have the property R, it is likely that all Xs have R (by [quantitative] induction). Second, since Q does have the properties P_1, P_2, P_3 and all Xs have those properties, it's likely that Q is a member of X (by [statistical] abduction). Therefore, since Q is probably a member of X and it's likely that all Xs have R, it is likely that Q has the property R (by [statistical] deduction).

Metaphoric reasoning (cf. CP 2.277, 2.222, 7.590, 1.383) should be distinguished from analogical reasoning (remember that Peirce makes a distinction between analogy and metaphor as different species of icons [CP 2.277]). As distinguished from analogical reasoning, metaphorical reasoning argues that two different kinds of things are, in a sense, the same thing because they share at least some properties, so that, for example, war might be used as a metaphor for argument or wine for blood. In other words, things of two *different* kinds (as opposed to analogical reasoning, where there is a comparison of things that are supposed to belong to the same kind) are parallel enough to warrant saying that in some sense they are of the same kind. Put differently, in analogy the goal is to show that certain things which share some characteristics with other things share some additional characteristics as well (a statistical induction) precisely because it is supposed that they belong to the same class or kind of thing (a statistical abduction). In metaphoric reasoning, on the other hand, the goal is to show that two things are, in a certain sense, of the same kind precisely because they share certain critical characteristics.[16] For that reason it can be seen as a mostly abductive process.[17] Indeed, one version of formal structure of abductive inference seems to capture this idea:

> A well-recognized kind of object, M, has for its ordinary predicates, P_1, P_2, P_3, indistinctly recognized.
> The suggesting object S, has these same predicates.
> Hence, S is of the kind M. (CP 8.64)

Peirce also mentions a number of other reasoning operations, including restriction, determination, descent, depletion, extension, prescision, abstraction, and ascent (CP 2.422–2.430), which also can characterize the sort of reasoning involved in observation (including coenoscopic observation). These too are divided into species of deductive or explicative types of reasoning and ampliative processes. The latter include *extension*, which is the discovery that a predicate applies to subjects to which it was not previously applied (CP 2.422n1). For example, principles of mechanics can be extended to the behavior of the atmosphere, or a theorem relating to plane curves can be modified so as to apply to all curves in space (CP 4.22n1). Consequently, extension involves an increase of breadth without change of depth. *Restriction* is the contrary of extension. It is a process of reasoning which allows us to say of a certain predicate that it belongs only to these members of a class and not others (cf. CP 2.427). Using extension as the model, restriction is the discovery that certain predicates which were thought to apply generally to a class of things apply only to certain members. We might say that dogs in general are domesticable animals; however, this does not apply to a certain species of dog (e.g., wolf hybrids).

Both restriction and extension deal primarily with the question of breadth of a proposition. Reasoning processes that are focused primarily on the increase and decrease of depth, respectively, are called *determination* and *depletion*. Determination is the process of reasoning by which we add greater and greater depth, more and more predicates to a particular subject (CP 2.422). A complete determination would involve a display of all the predicates that apply to some subject. A complete depletion, as we surmise, would be the subject understood without reference to any of its predicates, its mere facticity, so to speak, that it is "there." Depletion is the diminution of depth for certain purposes (CP 2.428). Thus an epidemiologist, for certain research purposes, might be interested only in the fact that an organism has AIDS and not in the fact that this organism is a human being.

Generalization or *ascent*, on the other hand, means the discovery, by reflection upon a number of cases, of a general description applicable to all those cases; it is a characterization derived from the comparison of a number of instances. For example, a definite conception of bookprinting in India in the nineteenth century is made on the basis of a comparison of a number of books from that period. It is not an induction, since it does not seek to establish the truth of the characterization, but involves the process of formulating that characterization—so it is akin to abduction; indeed, Peirce calls it *formal hypothesis* (CP 4.22n1). It has the following form:

> Since any M has a number of characteristics, C_1, C_2, C_3
> And since S is an M
> Therefore, S also has those characteristics

In this sense,[18] generalization is a combination of extension by depletion. That is to say, generalization allows us to say less about more things. By depleting certain predicates of a subject, the breadth of the subject can often be increased (cf. CP 2.429).

Descent or *specification* is the contrary of generalization. Descent allows us to say more about less; it increases the depth while at the same time restricting the breadth of the subject. It is not the same as determination, where we are able to say more about the subject without changing its breadth; nor is it simply restriction, since it is not just reducing the breadth of the subject. An example of descent might be the following: in assigning a number of predicates to dogs, descent would involve adding additional predicates to particular species of dogs which are not present in all dogs.

Hypostatic abstraction, as opposed to mental operations such as simple abstraction, prescision, discrimination, and dissociation, is considered to be a reasoning process, primarily a deductive one (CP 4.463, 4.332, 4.235). It is essentially the reasoning involved in moving from a perceptual judgment, such as "This is white," to the claim that "This possesses whiteness." In other words, it is a process of reasoning that leads to the supposition of a universal, the existence of "whiteness" as such (CP 4.463). Abstraction as a mental ability is essentially the contemplation of a form apart from matter (CP 2.428). This is different from prescision, which is the ability to think of a notion *indifferenter*, that is, to think of something without regard to the differences of its individuals, as when we think of a white thing generally (CP 2.428). Discrimination is the sensory ability which allows us to distinguish red from blue, space from color (although we cannot discriminate red from color) (CP 1.549). Dissociation is a psychological ability to regard two things that are thought together as also thought separately. We can dissociate red from blue, but we cannot dissociate blue from color (CP 1.549).

Specification is the contrary of generalization. It is the process of reasoning which allows us to gain more insight into a specific feature or predicate of a thing. Where generalization allows us to tell something about everything of a certain class (at the cost of specification of those predicates), specification allows us to say something in greater depth about a smaller number of things of the class.

The Process of Reasoning

The leading principles of the three principal modes of reasoning suggest that reasoning is performed within the nexus of inquiry; and inquiry is an ongoing process which interrelates abduction, deduction, and induction in a continuing cycle, with the idea that such a process, if continued indefinitely, would converge toward the truth of the matter investigated. As Peirce writes,

> [Pragmatism consists in] studying out what effect that hypothesis, if embraced, must have in modifying our expectations in regard to future experience. Thereupon we make experiments . . . in order to

find out how far these new conditional expectations are going to be fulfilled. In so far as they greatly modify our former expectations of experience and in so far as we find them . . . to be fulfilled, we accord to the hypothesis due weight in determining all our future conduct and thought . . . we have only to persist in this same method of research and we shall gradually be brought around to the truth. (CP 7.115)

More specifically, Peirce outlines this process in the following way:

That which is to be done with the hypothesis is to trace out its consequences by deduction, to compare them with results of experiment by induction, and to discard the hypothesis, and try another, as soon as the first has been refuted; as it presumably will be. How long it will be before we light upon the hypothesis which shall resist all tests we cannot tell; but we hope we shall do so, at last. (CP 7.220; cf. CP 2.96, 5.311, 5.170, 5.161)

When applied to the matter of scientific hypothesis, then, deduction, induction, and abduction play specific but interrelated roles. Abduction is concerned with the formation of a hypothesis; deduction in this context is concerned with drawing out the necessary consequences of such a hypothesis;[19] and induction is dedicated to determining whether such consequences actually occur.

Science is the most exemplary in this regard, but this process, it can be argued, is exhibited in all aspects of semeiosis. As an illustration of this process, consider the case of Roberta Janacek.[20] Janacek was referred by the Mayo Clinic to Dr. Harold Klawans, a specialist in Parkinson's disease. She had been under Mayo's care for nearly fifteen years, ever since Mayo physicians discovered and treated her hyperthyroid condition, a condition which required surgical removal of the thyroid. Recently they had diagnosed Parkinson's disease and were treating it with L-dopa, but still she was slowly deteriorating. Since Parkinson's patients typically respond well to such treatment, the doctors were puzzled and sent her to Klawans.

Her records described her as a patient with classic Parkinson's disease, and all patients so diagnosed had responded to L-dopa in Klawans's clinical experience. L-dopa is transformed in the brain into dopamine, a vital chemical that is lacking in Parkinson's patients. Normally dopamine is produced by a specific set of nerve cells in the substantia nigra, at the base of the brain. Dopamine is a neurotransmitter and allows the substantia nigra to control one of the major motor areas of the brain, the striatum. If there is no dopamine, the patient develops Parkinson's disease, although the striatum remains normal in such patients. Consequently, if the dopamine can be replaced by means of L-dopa, Parkinson's patients improve.

Klawans formulated four likely and plausible hypotheses that could account for the anomaly in Janacek's case. The first was that Janacek really didn't have Parkinson's disease after all but some other neurological malady. A second hypothesis suggested that sufficient L-dopa wasn't being administered. A third hypothesis suggested that she wasn't responding to L-dopa because of some possible side effects of the drug. The fourth was that she was suffering from hypothyroidism; a normal level of thyroid hormone is needed for the brain cells to respond to L-dopa, and given that her thyroid had been removed some years before, hypothyroidism could be a possibility.

Klawans determined the conditions under which each hypothesis could be easily tested. If the first hypothesis was the case, the typical clinical symptoms would be absent; if the second was the case, increasing the dosage should lead to an improvement; if the third, the substitution of lergotrile or bromocriptine for L-dopa should lead to some improvement; if the fourth, a check would show that the hormone level was below normal.

Upon clinical examination Janacek exhibited all the classical Parkinson symptoms: tremor, stiffness, slowness of movement, imbalance, loss of facial expression, slurred, monotonous speech, tight handwriting; there were no signs of any other neurological problems. So it seemed that the first hypothesis was not the case. A simple test result from the endocrinologist showed that the thyroid hormone level was normal, so the fourth hypothesis seemed implausible. Klawans then decided to increase the amount of L-dopa. Still there was no improvement, and the amount was further increased. Half a year went by and there was still no improvement. The second hypothesis seemed unlikely. He then decided on an alternative treatment: first bromocriptine, which after a trial period had no noticeable effect, then lergotrile; again, after a trial period there was no improvement. In fact, halfway through the trial Janacek had to start using a cane, and by its end she had to employ a walker.

All four hypotheses seemed bankrupt. Klawans had to come up with a new hypothesis. But first he decided to make sure that he had not missed anything in regard to the first four hypotheses, so he ordered more tests, including a spinal tap. The spinal tap would be an additional way of testing the first hypothesis, since it would tell how much dopamine Janacek's brain had lost. Since the spinal fluid bathes the brain and carries away many of the breakdown products of the chemicals that are active in the brain and dopamine, when broken down, produces a chemical called

HVA, the amount of HVA would be an indication of whether the dopamine was being processed. In Parkinson's disease the brain has less dopamine than normal, and the spinal fluid consequently has less HVA. The normal level of HVA is between 60 and 180 units, but in a Parkinson's patient it is usually below 20.

The result of the tap was a reading of 164 for HVA—well within the normal level. Another anomaly: patients with Parkinson's disease never have such a high level of HVA. The only hypothesis that could explain this anomaly was that Janacek did not have Parkinson's disease. It then dawned on Klawans that the problem might lie not with the transmitter cells of the substantia nigra but with the receptor cells of the striatum. If the striatal cells were not able to respond to dopamine, Janacek would look and act like a patient with Parkinson's disease, yet her HVA level would be normal because her brain was making sufficient dopamine.

Two hypotheses now suggested themselves to Klawans: hypothyroidism or hypoparathyroidism. The latter may result after thyroid surgery if the nearby parathyroid glands are accidentally injured. It sometimes shows up on skull x-rays as a tell-tale brain calcification. The test for the first hypothesis proved negative, but a CT scan, a test which had recently been developed at that time, showed exactly what Klawans feared—the striatum was completely calcified. There was no way that the striatum could receive the dopamine transmitters. His hypothesis was additionally confirmed by a test designed specifically for the parathyroid function.

Klawans attempted to treat the hypoparathyroid condition, but it was too late; nothing could dissolve the calcium patches. Janacek slowly deteriorated and died within three years.

Klawans's reasoning illustrates the interrelated, tripartite process of abduction-deduction-induction. It is the puzzling, anomalous event of Roberta Janacek's lack of response to L-dopa which prompts Klawans to propose the various hypotheses that *could* account for this anomaly. This reaction captures the process of abduction, as Peirce outlines it. Klawans then proceeds to design tests for each hypothesis; this reaction involves a process of deduction: if the hypothesis is the case, certain consequences should result. Klawans then engages in the actual testing of each of these plausible hypotheses; this reaction involves the process of induction. When each of the hypotheses fails, Klawans faces another anomaly, which he attempts to account for by proposing another hypothesis. In turn, he designs a test for the hypothesis; and when it succeeds, he seeks out other means of confirmation of that hypothesis, to the point where he feels relatively satisfied that the hypothesis has a high degree of credibility. The process can be expressed diagrammatically as a conical helix: as the reasoning processes interconnect and circle one another, the effort eventually rises to a point of best outcome.

The Validity of the Ultimate Leading Principles of the Three Forms of Reasoning

Establishing the validity of a form of reasoning is the means by which we can assure or guarantee that this process of reasoning is one that will lead to predominantly true conclusions. As Peirce puts it more concretely, the central question of logic is "just how is it that any record of events in the past can furnish any assurance . . . to assume of what the characters of future event to be" (MS 603: 8).

Such assurance is achieved when we can determine the validity of the argument or the validity of the ultimate leading principles of the type of argument. For Peirce, determining the validity of an argument hinges on determining the truth of its leading principle (CP 2.463). If one can guarantee the validity of a leading principle, then, given true premises, the conclusion will have a guarantee of being either necessarily or probably true, depending on the type of argument (CP 2.464). Let's look at the ultimate leading principles for the three basic types of reasoning.

The ultimate leading principle of deduction is that if a particular logical principle is valid, then in no analogous case will it lead to a false conclusion from true premises (CP 2.204, 2.267, 4.477; W 4: 246). In other words, the validity of a necessary inference depends on its tendency to generate true conclusions in all analogous circumstances.

The ultimate leading principle of induction is that a method such as induction, "if steadily adhered to, would at length lead to an indefinite approximation to the truth, or, at least, would assure the reasoner of ultimately attaining as close an approach to the truth as he can, in any way, be assured of attaining" (CP 2.204; cf. CP 1.93). The "law of large numbers" might be thought to be a corollary of this.[21] This simply suggests that, as in the case of quantitative induction, as the sample increases, an approximation to the characterization of the whole gets closer to the truth, just as when one expands pi, the number is a more accurate approximation of the ratio of the circumference to the diameter of a circle. In the case of qualitative induction, as the testable consequences of a hypothesis are confirmed, the approximation to the truth of the matter which that hypothesis addresses is reached to a corresponding degree.

The ultimate leading principle of abduction is that the human mind is akin to the truth in the sense that in a finite number of guesses it will light upon the correct hypothesis (CP 5.172, 5.173).[22] In other words, given enough minds, effort, and time, inquirers generally will discover the correct hypothesis.

If one carefully considers these three leading principles, it becomes clear that they are all intimately connected with Peirce's convergence theory of truth; in fact, they are simply axioms of that account. If truth is what corresponds to the final outcome of a process of inquiry informed by reasoning processes that result for the most part in attaining truth, that is, if truth is a process of convergence, then it must be presupposed that there are methods of reasoning which, when applied to the matter at hand, yield a good result.

Peirce claims that these ultimate leading principles of reasoning cannot be justified by any empirical fact nor by any inference (since inferences are themselves grounded in the ultimate leading principles; CP 5.347). Instead, the synthetic inferences of abduction and induction especially can only be valid if in fact something like a process of inquiry is possible. What makes induction and abduction ultimately valid is the claim that inquiry, if pursued by these types of inferences, will ultimately light upon the truth; yet our faith in inquiry as a means of truth convergence rests in the confidence in these types of inferences. This circularity is neatly expressed by Peirce:

> As all knowledge comes from synthetic inference, we must equally infer that all human certainty consists merely in our knowing that the processes by which our knowledge has been derived are such as must generally have led to true conclusions. (CP 2.693)

Put differently, one might say that the ultimate leading principle which validates induction is itself an induction. The circularity can be broken only by saying that if anything will succeed in truth convergence, it would be a inductionlike principle. In this case, one might think of Peirce's claim here as transcendental in the Kantian sense, that is, the very condition of the possibility of truth is the condition cited by ultimate leading principles. But Peirce seems to want to avoid this sort of transcendental reasoning[23] simply because of his distrust of a priori language (CP 5.383), so that ultimately the ultimate leading principles themselves must be considered fallible and so subject to question. However, at the same time, there is no reason, given the factual progress of science, to engage in an artificial, Cartesian exercise of doubt about them. The only other possibility is to suggest another strategy analogous to one Kant performs in the first critique. Whereas, for Kant, certain theoretical claims, such as the existence of God, the freedom of the will, and the immortality of the soul, cannot be proved by theoretical reason, nonetheless they serve as practical postulates; that is, for morality to be possible, freedom of the will must be practically presupposed; without free will morality makes no sense. Similarly, Peirce's ultimate leading principles cannot be justified either by themselves or by the patterns of reason they validate but are justified in the *practice* of inquiry. They must be *presupposed* in order to have anything like inquiry (cf. W 2: 272).[24] Indeed, there is an uncanny resemblance between Kant's argument for the immortality of the soul as a practical postulate and Peirce's notion of the indefinite community of inquirers (cf. CP 5.311). Kant argues that the achievement of the highest good is the complete fitness of the will to the moral law, that is, holiness. Its possibility requires an endless progress to that complete fitness. "This infinite progress is possible, however, only under the presupposition of an infinitely enduring existence and personality of the same rational being; this is called the immortality of the soul."[25] Peirce has a more collective, communal version of this argument. Substitute "knowledge of the real" for "holiness" and "community" for "personality," and the same argument is made in Peirce: "Thus, the very origin of the conception of reality shows that this conception essentially involves the notion of a COMMU-NITY, without definite limits, and capable of a definite increase of knowledge" (CP 5.311). Thus the notion of the real *must presuppose* an indefinite community of inquiry. Consequently, the leading principles articulated by critical logic find their ultimate ground in universal rhetoric, which, in its most comprehensive sense, is the study of the formal conditions for the *practice* of inquiry within a community.

4 Universal Rhetoric

Universal or speculative rhetoric is the least developed branch of Peirce's general semeiotic theory.[1] This makes it the most difficult to interpret. However, it is not undeveloped in the sense that there is no material on that topic in Peirce, but rather that, unlike the other branches of semeiotic, there is no exact map to follow. Once it is understood what Peirce means by universal rhetoric, it becomes clear that a great deal of his work is dedicated to it. In fact, universal rhetoric permeates Peirce's entire corpus of work, but it is not collected together in any systematic fashion, and there are many loose threads.

What is surprising is that Peirce did not prioritize this branch of semeiotic given the importance he assigns to it. He proclaims it to be "the highest and most living branch of logic" (CP 2.333) and that it would "lead to the most important philosophical conclusions" (CP 3.454).[2]

Peirce gives a number of different characterizations of universal rhetoric (otherwise known as *speculative rhetoric* [MS 774: 7–8], *general rhetoric* [MS 346: 3], *formal rhetoric* [CP 1.559], *objective logic* [NEM 4: 26–31], or *methodeutic* [NEM 4: 62]), and these differ enough so that a general characterization of the subject matter is somewhat problematic. In order to make these various characterizations coherent, a distinction has to be made between universal rhetoric in its general, more formal sense and in its narrower sense. It can be argued that the most satisfactory general definition of universal rhetoric is the following: "the doctrine of the general conditions of the reference of symbols and other signs to the Interpretants which they determine" (CP 2.93, MS 793: 20); or, as he puts it even more broadly, "the science of the essential conditions under which a sign may determine an interpretant sign of itself and of whatever it signifies, or may, as a sign bring about a physical result" (MS 774: 5). This gives it a flavor similar to the other two branches of semeiotic. Semeiotic grammar is concerned with the formal conditions of signs qua signs, that is, the formal conditions which will make something count as a sign. Critical logic, on the other hand, is concerned with the formal conditions under which a symbol can be counted as being true, that is, the relation between symbols and their objects. Comparatively, then, universal rhetoric can be thought of as the formal conditions for *attainment* of truth (CP 2.207),[3] that is, the relation between signs and their interpretants.

In its narrower sense, universal rhetoric can be thought of simply as the study of the formal or logical conditions of inquiry (cf. CP 2.106, MS L75); "the doctrine of how truth must be properly investigated, or is capable of being ascertained" (MS 320: 27; cf. MS 606: 15, CP 1.191); the "ordering and arranging of inquiries (MS 452: 9). This also harmonizes well with the goals of semeiotic grammar and critical logic. Critical logic, as the study of right inference, requires, in turn, an analysis of inquiry, understood as a cooperative investigation aimed at the truth, a sort of *coduction*, to use a term coined by Wayne Booth.[4] As the preceding chapter emphasized, all the leading principles of critical logic depend on the idea of inquiry, that is, an indefinitely extended and cooperative investigation into the truth, the so-called social principle of logic (CP 5.354). It is clear, then, that critical logic is dependent upon universal rhetoric as the study of the formal conditions of inquiry.

If universal rhetoric is understood in its formal and general sense as the relation between signs and their interpretants, it could be thought to have, in principle, three divisions:[5] one in regard to the relation of signs to their immediate interpretants, a second in relation to the dynamic interpretant, and the third in relation to the final interpretant. Since Peirce sees a similarity between his three types of interpretants and Lady Welby's notions of the *sense, meaning*, and *significance* of the sign (cf. NEM 3: 844; LW 110–111, 80), we might adopt her terminology in labeling these divisions.

Sense, or the *result* of the sign's *relation* to its immediate interpretant, could be thought of as the immediate intelligibility of the sign (cf. LW 110). It is identified with the effect the sign first produces or may produce upon a mind, without any reflection upon it (LW 110). Sense could be understood in its broadest terms as "the effect of a Sign as would enable a person to say whether or not the Sign was applicable to anything concerning which that person had sufficient acquaintance" (LW 110). Thus some definitions of universal rhetoric seem to address this particular aspect: it is the "fundamental conditions of the intelligibility of symbols" (MS 340: 34, WP 1: 175; cf. MS 774: 9–11) or the "power of symbols of appealing to a mind" (CP 4.116, 1.559).

Meaning is established in the sign's *relation* to its dynamic inter- pretant; it is the direct effect that the sign has on the sign-interpreting agency, its ability to impart something to that agency about its dynamic object or, in a literal sense, to in-form the agency (cf. MS 793), to provide information to sign-interpreting agencies. In other terms, mean- ing is established in the sign's ability to *actually determine*, in the sign-interpreting agency, an interpretant which translates the dynamic object's determination of the sign. Universal rhetoric, in this regard, can be thought of as the "study of the necessary conditions of the transmission of meaning by signs from mind to mind, from one state of mind to another" (CP 1.445; cf. CP 2.93); or "the study of the practical consequences of accepting the belief of a proposition" (NEM 4: 291); or, most generally, the study of rendering signs effective (MS 774: 2); "to ascertain precisely what it is that renders it possible for us in reasoning one fact or pair of facts, straightaway to recognize that another proposition is true" (MS 637: 18).

Significance is the *result* of the sign's *relation* to its final and ultimate interpretant. It is primarily concerned with not only the systematic and inferential growth and development of signs, but also the *significant effects* such signs have on sign interpreting agencies. So it is also concerned with the establishment of habits in these agencies. There are a number of char- acterizations of universal rhetoric which pertain to this aspect: it is con- cerned with the conditions pertinent to the determination of an ultimate interpretant (NEM 4: 62); it studies the growth of Reason in the history of the human mind (NEM 4: 30–31); the theory of the advancement of knowl- edge of all kind (MS 449: 56); the study of the influence of ideas in the physical world (NEM 4: 31); it "looks to the purposed ultimate interpretant and inquires what conditions a sign must conform to, in order to be perti- nent to the purpose" (NEM 4: 62); "the science of the general laws of [symbols'] relations to other systems of symbols (MS 346[G-1864-3]: 3); the doctrine of the evolution of thought; the nature of teleological action

(CP 2.108); the general doctrine of methods of attaining purposes in general (CP 2.108); the study of "life in Signs," their order of development (CP 2.111). The connection between the formal conditions of sense, meaning, and significance and the more specific sense of universal rhetoric as the formal study of inquiry can be made in the following way. Keeping in mind that the interpretant is understood as process, product, and effect, then the sense, meaning, and significance of signs should be understood from each of these three aspects. For example, in regard to final and ultimate interpretant understood as a *significant process*, this suggests inquiry as the primary means by which signs grow and develop; inquiry, as opposed to formal inference, is a communal process, a practice or form of conduct, that is ongoing and develops and grows over time; it requires the cooperation of a number of individuals and must take place within the context of certain communities which can engender it. The *product* of inquiry is the establishment of *true* belief or *knowledge*, the settlement of opinion, or *consensus* (cf. CP 6.610) in a general sense. The *effect* of the establishment of true belief is self-control (CP 5.433) or, for the general population, behavior that exhibits a concrete reasonableness (CP 5.3).

As a *process*, meaning is *communication* (cf. LW 196 f.), either among sign-interpreting agents, such as human communication, or among thoughts within the same agent, or intraagency communication, or between agents and nonagents, in the sense in which nature may transmit (through indices) certain information about itself (cf. CP 6. 158). The *product* of communication is *information*; the *effect* of communication is *understanding*, in the sense of a shared common understanding, in the case of interhuman communication (cf. LW 197).

The *products* of sense are things such as feelings, sentiments, impressions, intuitions, instincts, ideas, intelligibility.[6] Collectively they form a sort of common sense (cf. CP 1.654, 8.179), a universe of discourse (CP 4.172) or common ground, what Peirce sometimes calls the *commens* of the sign agency, which serves as the basis or the core of the agent's habits of action (LW 197).[7] They are the result of a *process* of continuous sign translation of which the sign-interpreting agency is a part and shares with others within that continuum, that is, a *community*. The *effect* is to create a certain *sensibility* or *comprehensibility* (CP 4.117) in the interpreting agencies who share that same continuum of sign translation.

The general and the narrower character of universal rhetoric combine to suggest that the most immediate task of universal rhetoric is the establishment of the formal conditions for community, communication, and inquiry. However, the approach in universal rhetoric cannot be as formal as the other two branches, and for the following reason. From the perspective of semeiotic grammar, although most signs have an utterer and an interpreter, each is irrelevant to the analysis of sign relations. Consequently, the results of semeiotic grammar are relevant to any sign process no matter whether there are utterers or interpreters and regardless of the sort of sign-interpreting agency involved; for example, the interpretant, in this context, must be understood "apart from its context and circumstances of utterance" (CP 5.473). To a certain degree the same could be said of critical logic. It establishes norms for inferencing by which, independently of any sign-interpreting agency, some sign-interpreting agency would be able by means of their exercise to arrive at the truth in the long run. But it is clear at the same time that not any kind of sign-interpreting agency is capable of inference, understood in a normative sense as self-corrective; rather, that requires a certain sort of sign agency, one that is capable of *"scientific"* intelligence:

> Triadic relations . . . are essentially open to evaluation; a sign may represent its object to its interpreter rightly or wrongly, truly or falsely, better or worse. These normative terms imply the possibility of correction and improvement. It is an essential property of semeiosis, therefore, that it can be corrected and improved upon. . . . (CP 1.124)

Consequently, critical logic seems to be directed to certain sorts of sign agencies, those capable of scientific intelligence, that is, self-correction in the form of inquiry.

Similarly, it seems that universal rhetoric, although it is concerned with the formal conditions for community, communication, and inquiry, must be concerned to some extent with those types of scientific intelligence capable of community and communication (cf. CP 2.229). Peirce says, "in coming to Speculative Rhetoric, after the main conceptions of logic have been well settled, there can be no serious objection to relaxing the severity of our rule of excluding psychological matter, observations of how we think, and the like" (CP 2.107; but see the qualification in CP 4.117).

The Formal Conditions for Community

Critical logic, as the study of right inference, requires, in turn, an analysis of inquiry, understood as a cooperative investigation aimed at the truth, a sort of coduction. All the leading principles of critical logic depend on the idea of inquiry, that is, an indefinitely extended and cooperative investigation into the truth, the so-called social principle of logic. It is clear that critical logic is dependent upon universal rhetoric as the study of the formal conditions of inquiry. Inquiry requires a community (of the right sort) as the essential context in which inquiry proceeds; thus, in part, universal rhetoric is the study of the formal conditions of community.

Critical logic is the study of the formal conditions of truth. The notion of truth supposes that there is a reality. The real as Peirce defines it is *represented* in the final opinion, that is, the ultimate consensus of an indefinite community of inquirers. Consequently, the very notion of the real and the possibility of inquiry is connected to the notion of community: " . . . the very origin of the conception of reality shows that this conception essentially involves the notion of a COMMUNITY, without definite limits, and capable of a definite increase of knowledge" (CP 5.311). Consequently, "the social principle is rooted intrinsically in logic" (CP 5.354, 2.654):

> The very idea of probability and of reasoning rests on the assumption that this number [of inferences] is indefinitely great. . . . It seems to me that we are driven to this, that logicality inexorably requires that our interests shall *not* be limited. They must not stop at our own fate, but must embrace the whole community. This community, again, must not be limited, but must extend to all races of beings with whom we can come into immediate or mediate intellectual relation. It must reach, however, vaguely, beyond this geological epoch, beyond all bounds. (CP 2.654)

In one sense, then, a community requires that its members be capable of coming into an immediate or mediate intellectual relation; in other words, the first formal condition of having a community is that its members are capable of mediative or sign-interpreting capacity to some degree.[8] Second, there must be some connection or relation, especially a communicative one, between such sign users. Third, this passage suggests that this connection or relation must be established as "ours" in some sense, that is, there must be some identification with this relation on the part of those so related. The first condition allows the possibility of the second, since signs enable us to transform objects or events into meanings, which in turn allow the possibility of something being shared and shared in a communicative fashion. The second condition allows for the possibility of the third, since identifying shared meanings as "ours" assumes that there is, first of all, something that *can* be shared.

The second condition seems to be established by means of the very nature of semeiosis as a continuous, synechistic process. The principle of synechism, as applied to thought-signs generally, states "that ideas tend to spread continuously and to affect certain others which stand to them in a peculiar relation of affectability. In this spreading they lose intensity, and especially the power of affecting others, but gain generality and become welded with other ideas" (CP 6.104). Three aspects are involved in the "affection" of signs: "the first is its intrinsic quality as a feeling. The second is the energy with which it affects other ideas. . . . The third element is the tendency of an idea to bring along other ideas with it" (CP 6.135). The idea of a singular thought, a singular sign, is a fiction; all signs are the result of previous ones, each sign has a history, a tradition behind it. Sign activity is a process, a semeiosis, governed by the principle of synechism or continuity: " . . . there is no intuition or cognition not determined by previous cognitions. . . . [it] is an *event* occupying time, and coming to pass by a continuous process. . . . there is no moment at which there is a thought belonging to this series, subsequently to which there is not a thought which interprets or repeats it. There is no exception, therefore, to the law that every thought-sign is translated or interpreted in a subsequent one, unless it be that all thought comes to an abrupt and final end in death" (CP 5.284).

The very act of having a thought-sign, understood in the most generous sense, implies a continuity with signs, especially symbols, that have preceded it as well as those which will now anticipate it:

> At any moment we are in possession of certain information, that is, of cognitions which have been logically derived by induction and hypothesis from previous cognitions which are less general, less distinct, and of which we have a less lively consciousness. These in their turn have been derived from others still less general, less distinct, and less vivid; and so on back to the ideal first, which is quite singular, and quite out of consciousness. (CP 5.311)

A sign is not a singular, isolated event but is a translation *from* previous signs and serves as the translation *into* others. Thus every agency capable of signs must be, in some sense, connected to this continuous process. The capability of having an interpretant already implies that one is connected to a continuous process of sign translation. The words a person (or any other sign agency) uses, the thoughts she thinks, the signs she employs, have a history, are the result of a continuous translation process; but they also have a future to which the person is joined; that is, they have a tendency to connect to others. In both cases, by the very act of sign use, a sign-interpreting agency is intrinsically related to other sign users. *Sign and community are inherently correlative.* The partition of a *particular* community from others is simply the act of identifying with part of this larger continuum, of attaching to it special significance or sentiment. But the very possibility of *any* community is the continuity, the synechism which the sign process engenders. This formal condition for community is nicely expressed by Josiah Royce, the contemporary of Peirce, whose later writing is expressly influenced by Peirce's theory of signs:[9]

> The *first* condition upon which the existence of a community, in our sense of the word, depends, is the power of an individual self to extend his life, in ideal fashion, so as to regard it as including past and future events which lie far away in time, and which he does not now personally remember. That his power exists, and that man has a self which is thus ideally extensible in time without any definable limit we all know. This power itself rests upon the principle that, however a man may come by his idea of himself, the self is no mere datum, but is in its essence a life which is interpreted, and which interprets itself, and which, apart from some sort of ideal interpretation, is a mere flight of ideas, or a meaningless flow of feelings, or a vision that sees nothing, or else a barren abstract conception.[10]

To the extent that sign-interpreting agencies qua sign-using agency are part of this continuous translation of sign, which constitutes their experience in a generous sense, communication among such sign users is possible. As Peirce argues, "all communication from mind to mind is through continuity of being" (CP 7.572).[11]

The third condition which Peirce suggests makes a community possible is that sign-interpreting agencies come to *share* some aspect of this continuous process, that is, in some sense not only become translators for one another but also to some degree identify with some aspect of the continuum:

> The course of life has developed certain compulsions of thought which we speak of collectively as Experience. Moreover, the inquirer more or less vaguely identifies himself in sentiment with a Community of which he is a member, and which includes, for example, besides his momentary self, his self of ten years hence; and he speaks of the resultant cognitive compulsions of the course of life of the community as Our Experience. (CP 8.101)[12]

Again, Royce states this condition nicely:

> The third of the conditions for the existence of the community which my definition emphasizes consists in the fact that the ideally extended past and future selves of the members include at least

some events which are, for all these selves, identical. This third condition is the one which furnishes both the most exact, the most widely variable, and the most important of the motives which warrant us in calling a community a real unit.[13]

In addition to the formal conditions for community, universal rhetoric in its more practical aspect and considered at the level of sense is concerned to cultivate a certain sensibility in members of a community which makes them more conducive to the practice of inquiry and to provide the conditions in the community which best allow inquiry to proceed. Thus universal rhetoric might be concerned in part with a characterization of those "logical" sentiments necessary and conducive to the practice of inquiry (CP 5.357) and in part with the characterization of the community most suitable for the practice of inquiry. To put it simply, in order that inquiry can take place, not only must there be a community, but it must be a community of a certain sort. (This question is more properly concerned with the nature of inquiry, and so will be dealt with later.) But, further, not only must the community be of a certain sort; its members must *desire* to see inquiry flourish, that is, they must have cultivated a certain sensibility toward inquiry.

Since Peirce was greatly influenced by Schiller (CP 2.197), we might think of cultivation in his sense, as a certain aesthetic education, the creation of a sensibility that makes morality and rationality possible.[14] This includes Schiller's idea of *Spieltrieb*,[15] or the "play impulse," which Peirce calls "the play of musement" (cf. CP 6.458 ff.). The essence of the play of musement is the liberty it entails, the freedom to think, to play with thought, which is crucial to the development of ideas (cf. CP 6.460). Thus the cultivation of this play, this freedom of thought, is critical for a community interested in inquiry. Overall, then, just as Peirce sees part of the job of critical logic as the cultivation of good thinking, he sees universal rhetoric, in part, as the cultivation of right habits and sentiments conducive to thinking and inquiry.[16] Its goal is the cultivation of certain sentiments, the construction of a certain *Weltanschauung* (CP 2.118).

What sort of sentiments should be present in members of a certain community in order to allow inquiry to flourish?

> . . . I . . . put forward three sentiments, namely, interest in an indefinite community, recognition of the possibility of this interest being made supreme, and hope in the unlimited continuance of intellectual activity, as indispensable requirements of logic. (CP 2.655)[17]

It seems that, first, there has to be some sense of supraindividualism, that is, some sensibility toward collective good. An individual must be willing, at least in part, to see her interests bound up with the interests of the indefinite community and willing to play a role in that regard:

> The question whether the *genus homo* has any existence except as individuals, is the question whether there is anything of any more dignity, worth and importance than individual happiness, individual aspirations, and individual life. Whether men really have anything in common, so that the *community* is to be considered as an end in itself, and if so, what the relative value of the two factors is [individual and community] is the most fundamental practical question in regard to every public institution the constitution of which we have it in our power to influence. (CP 8.38)

Inquiry "requires a conceived identification of one's interests with those of an unlimited community" (CP 2.654). In other words, there must be a "social impulse" (CP 2.655) present in the members of the community, "a generalized conception . . . which completes your personality by melting it into the neighboring parts of the universal cosmos" (CP 1.673). It involves the cultivation of the very sense of community, the realization that we are "mere cells of the social organism" (CP 1.673). "Logic is rooted in the social principle" (CP 2.654).

But if these are the sentiments that are necessary for inquiry, another consideration is the *desire* for the end of inquiry—that is, truth and reasonableness itself. This desire is modeled in the "ideal scientific man":

> The scientific man is deeply impressed with the majesty of truth, as something reasonable or intelligible which is bound sooner or later to force itself upon every mind. It is not too much to say that he worships the divine majesty of the power of reasonableness behind the fact. From that sentiment springs his ardent desire to further the discovery of truth. (CP 8.136n3)

In general, Peirce stresses the inherently admirable quality of reasonableness, as the springboard of inquiry: "The only desirable object which is quite satisfactory in itself without any ulterior reason for desiring it, is the reasonable itself" (CP 8.140). The admiration of this ideal dovetails with the social impulse:

> I do not see how one can have a more satisfying ideal of the admirable than the development of Reason so understood. The one thing whose admirableness is not due to an ulterior reason is Reason itself comprehended in all its fullness, so far as we can comprehend it.

Under this conception, the ideal of conduct will be to execute our little function in the operation of the creation by giving a hand toward rendering the world more reasonable. . . . (CP 1.615)

The importance of aesthetics, understood as the study of the admirable, is evident. For this reason, aesthetics serves as a foundational science for this aspect of universal rhetoric.

Peirce suggests that persons who have adopted these sentiments and ideals will have adopted certain presuppositions (CP 2.125–2.133):

1.   that there is such a thing as truth;
2.   not only is there truth, but it can be found out;
3.   truth can be found out primarily by reasoning about it;
4.   it is possible for a person (including yourself) to err and to be deceived;
5.   reasoning is superior to other means of settling opinion.

On the whole, inquiry is possible when there is, first, a community, second, whose members have acquired certain sentiments, ideals, and opinions conducive to inquiry, and, third, where the fundamental structure of the community itself fits the needs of the practice of inquiry (to be considered shortly).

Universal Rhetoric as the Formal Study of Communication

Critical logic alone is not sufficient to account for the nature of communication. Critical logic is primarily concerned with the truth of propositions, understood as the result of certain inferential processes; but critical logic is not capable of articulating the conditions under which propositions can be communicated or understood.[18] Yet, in order for inquiry and consensus to be successful, communication, especially communication of a certain sort, must be possible. Consequently, one of the goals of universal rhetoric is to account for the conditions which make communication possible.[19]

Essentially communication occurs when sign agencies can interchangeably, that is, dialogically as "utterer" and "interpreter," play the role of sign for each other. Each agency must, then, be capable of being a sign, since a sign acts as a medium for communication (LW 196).[20] So human beings, for example, are quite capable of communication, since after all "man [is] a sign" (CP 5.309), or two thoughts can communicate with one another since thoughts are signs (CP 5.283). Only those sign agencies capable of some triadic action are capable of genuine communication (although those that are not might be capable of degenerate forms of communication, that is, transmission of information without understanding).[21] It must be understood, then, that it is not so much the agency per se but the agency qua sign that makes communication possible (cf. MS 318: 79).

Extrapolating a bit on the few passages directly devoted to the topic of communication, Peirce seems to suggest the following formal conditions for communication:

1. There must be an utterer and interpreter.
2. There must be something transmitted between utterer and interpreter.
3. What is transmitted between utterer and interpreter must be something which is capable of establishing common interpretants in both utterer and interpreter. (Cf. LW 196 f.)[22]

Let me elaborate on each condition. Peirce makes it clear that in order for communication to take place there have to be two "subjects" (or perhaps the same subject at two different phases), one which "embodies" what is communicated prior to the communication and one that embodies it as a consequence of the communication (LW 196). The first, we assume, counts as the utterer, the second as the interpreter. The necessity of utterer and interpreter is mentioned elsewhere (cf. CP 4.551), although they are named "quasi-utterer" and "quasi-interpreter" to emphasize their more generic, possibly nonhuman characteristics. However, although other passages seem to reemphasize this condition (cf. MS 318: 79–80), they suggest that the essential condition for communication is not utterer or interpreter per se as a sign-interpreting agency but the utterer and interpreter as place holders, so to speak, for signs and interpretants.[23] In other words, utterers and interpreters are necessary to the extent that there must be some agencies capable of triadic interaction with a sign in order for communication to take place between them. This can be spelled out in the following way. Each communicating agency must be capable of at least the following, which corresponds to the formal properties of a sign: (1) The agency must be capable of being determined by an object. As Peirce suggests, in order for communication to be possible, the form or feature of an object must be embodied in a subject, independently of the communication (LW 196). An agency must be such that an object can establish in it something which can act as a sign of that object. (2) The correlative of this is the capability of the agency to represent the object in this regard. According to Peirce, the essential ingredient of the utterer is the function of standing for or representing the object (MS 318: 79). Simply put, when a person utters a word, or a dog barks, or a bee dances, it acts in that respect as a sign in its capacity to represent the object which has determined that sign. (3) Each agency must be capable of being determined by a sign, that is, of having an interpretant established within it (cf. MS 318: 79-80). In this context, the utterer is capable of engendering what Peirce calls an *intentional interpretant* (LW 196), that is, the sign which the utterer is, is in some sense intended or designed for the purpose of communication, and the interpreter is capable of engendering what he calls an *effectual interpretant*, that is, the interpreter can be affected by the sign that the utterer is.

The first condition infers, conversely, that if there is no utterer or interpreter, so defined, then communication cannot take place. Although Peirce is not entirely clear on this matter, he seems to hint at this in the following passage: " . . . natural Signs and symptoms have no utterer and consequently have no Meaning, if Meaning be defined as the intention of the utterer" (LW 111). I don't think Peirce intends to say that natural signs have no meaning, since surely the fever means something to the attending physician; rather he seems to be suggesting that natural signs, like the footprint of a moose in the snow, are not, in that context, part of any quasi-mind, and so are meaningless, that is, not capable of having an interpretant. In a sense the footprint in the snow, left unto itself, is a purely dyadic relation, and that's why it has no meaning, simply because it is a dyadic, causal relation between the foot of the moose and snow. The snow, so to speak, is not capable of having a triadic relation with the moose's foot, just as, in an example Peirce gives, the rise of the mercury in an ordinary thermometer is the result of the atmospheric temperature acting upon it "in a purely brute and dyadic way" (CP 5.473). However, when a mental representation of the index is produced, a triadic relation is established which would allow that dyadic relation to be incorporated into a triadic one (cf. CP 5.473). Should the footprint in the snow determine something in an agency capable of having a triadic relation with it, then it becomes a sign, and so becomes meaningful at that point. The relation between the footprint in the snow and the hunter, let's say, is not between utterer and interpreter, since the snow is not capable of forming an interpretant from the moose's foot. Consequently, there is, in a sense, a *transmission* of form or character to the hunter by means of the footprint in the snow, but no *communication*, strictly speaking. Communication occurs only if the utterer is capable of engendering an *intentional inter-*

pretant and the interpreter is capable of engendering an *effectual interpretant*.

The second condition, that there must be a transmission between utterer and interpreter, is articulated in the following terms by Peirce. He argues that what is transmitted in the act of communication is the form or feature of the object which is embodied in the utterer. By "form" he means something like the ground of the sign. "In order that a Form may be extended or communicated, it is necessary that it should have been really embodied in a Subject independently of the communication; and it is necessary that there should be another subject in which the same form is embodied only in consequence of the communication" (LW 196). But the simple transmission of "form" is not sufficient to establish communication, unless the form that is communicated is capable of establishing an interpretant in the interpreter which, in some sense, is similar to what is possible for the utterer. This leads to the third condition.

This third condition might be called the *dialogic* one. The sign that is transmitted can establish an interpretant in the interpreter somewhat similar to its establishment in the utterer. In other words, communication occurs when the utterer and interpreter can be "welded" by the transmitted sign: " . . . although these two [quasi-utterer and quasi-interpreter] are at one (i.e., *are* one mind) in the sign itself, they must nevertheless be distinct. In the Sign they are, so to say, *welded*. Accordingly, it is not merely a fact of human Psychology, but a necessity of Logic, that every logical evolution of thought should be dialogic" (CP 4.551). The "welding" or "fusing" (LW 196) of the utterer and interpreter in communication is expressed by what he calls the *cominterpretant* (LW 196). The cominterpretant is a *determination* of the *commens*, "it consists of all that is, and must be, well understood between utterer and interpreter at the outset, in order that the sign in question should fulfill its function" (LW 197). Generally speaking, one could argue, I think, that the commens is simply the *sense* of the *community* of experience shared commonly between utterer and interpreter, *sense* understood in its broadest terms: "the effect of A Sign as would enable a person to say whether or not the Sign was applicable to anything concerning which that person had sufficient acquaintance" (LW 110).[24] There seems to be some similarity between the notion of the commens and Peirce's concept of the *universe of discourse*. Peirce defines the latter in the following way: "in every proposition the circumstances of its enunciation show that it refers to some collection of individuals or of possibilities, which cannot be adequately described, but can only be indicated as something familiar to both speaker and auditor" (CP 2.536). The universe of discourse, the familiarity with a world, is acquired through

collateral experience, "the previous acquaintance with that the sign denotes" (CP 8.179). Thus to understand the proposition "Hamlet was mad"
"one must know that men are sometimes in that strange state; one must
have seen madmen or read about them; and it will be all the better if one
specifically knows . . . what Shakespeare's notion of insanity was" (CP
8.179). The universe of discourse is what an utterer and interpreter must
share in order for communication to result, and so might be more
appropriately called a *discourse community*. In order for genuine communication to take place the sign which is the utterer must be part of a sense
common to the interpreter, and *conversely; it requires a sensibility gained
from a common community*. This allows in principle the *exchangeability*
of utterer and interpreter, that is, the interpreter could in turn serve as the
utterer to the utterer. Peirce hints at this in the following passage:

> Let him [the utterer] try to specify a place on the interpreter's pan-
> orama, and he can only look over his own panorama, where he can
> find nothing but his own ideas. On that panorama he has, however,
> no difficulty in finding the interpreter's life, that is to say, his idea of
> it, and among the interpreter's panorama to which he conceives this
> scrap should be attached and this he expresses in his sign for the
> interpreter's benefit. The latter has to go through a similar round-
> about process to find a place in his own life that seems to corre-
> spond with his idea of the utterer's idea of his life and with all these
> changes of costume there is such imminent danger of mistake. . . .
> (MS 318L: 198–199)

The "changes of costume" create, the possibility of dialogue, that is,
corrective interchange, something that is absolutely critical for the possibility of inquiry.

The determination of this commens is the cominterpretant; through
the communication, a determination of the commens between utterer and
interpreter is made in some respect. If the determination is successful, it
yields an understanding between utterer and interpreter, the "welding" or
"fusing" which Peirce describes. It might be something as simple as
determining what is referred to in the sign communicated:

> A man, tramping along a weary and solitary road, meets an individ-
> ual of strange mien, who says, "There was a fire in Megara." If this
> should happen in the Middle United States, there might very likely
> be some village in the neighborhood called Megara. Or it may refer
> to one of the ancient cities of Megara, or to some romance. And the
> time is wholly indefinite. In short, nothing at all is conveyed until
> the person addressed asks, Where?—"Oh about half a mile along

there" pointing to whence he came. "And when?" "As I passed." Now an item of information has been conveyed, because it has been stated relatively to a well understood common experience. (LW 197)

"No object can be denoted unless it be put into relation to the object of the *commens*" (LW 197). Successful communication is the determination of that aspect of the commens transmitted in the communication, and communication is possible only if there is some commens, some community between utterer and interpreter:

> The universe [referred to in a proposition] must be well known and mutually known to be known and agreed to exist, in some sense, between speaker and hearer, between the mind as appealing to its own further consideration and the mind as so appealed to, or there can be no communication, or "common ground" at all. (CP 3.621)

The Teleology of Communication

The goal of communication is to achieve a complete determination of that aspect of the commens or universe of discourse transmitted in the communication:

> Honest people, when not joking, intend to make the meaning of their words determinate, so that there shall be no latitude of interpretation at all. That is to say, the character of their meaning consists in the implications and non-implications of their words; and they intend to fix what is implied and what is not implied. (CP 5.447)

The goal of communication is to achieve "no latitude of interpretation" (CP 5.447). Put differently, understanding, or the "fusion" of utterer and interpreter, is achieved when the sign that is transmitted has created similar interpretants in both utterer and interpreter. Dialogically, this means that each can agree to the other's interpretation of the sign. Zero latitude of interpretation means a consensus of meaning between interpreter and utterer. The dialogic process, which involves the interchangeability of roles made possible by the commens between utterer and interpreter, involves a corrective interchange that fixes the determination. We can think of the communicative process as similar to the process of inquiry, as mapped by a conical helix, that is, a movement which spirals upward to a fixed point, a point which represents complete determination, where there is no longer a latitude of interpretation between utterer and interpreter.

The dialogic process, in this respect, is characterized by Peirce as a set of implicit or explicit norms, rules, roles, duties, and obligations to be performed by the utterer or interpreter, in a way that anticipates speech-act theory.[25] To clarify this a bit, one could say that since the purpose of communication is to achieve determination of the transmission, then, conversely, its goal is to eliminate indeterminacy. Indeterminacy is of two types, according to Peirce: vagueness (indefiniteness) and generality (CP 5.448n1), vagueness being the antithetical analogue of generality (CP 5.505). Within the context of a dialogue between utterer and interpreter, generality leaves further determination to the interpreter of the sign (CP 5.505, 5.447). On the other hand, in the case of vagueness, "the right of determination is not distinctly extended to the interpreter [but] it remains the right of the utterer" (CP 5.506). To put it differently, "a definite proposition is one the assertor of which leaves himself no loophole for escape against attack by saying that he did not mean so and so, but something else" (MS 515: 25).

Indeterminacy in a proposition can be an indeterminacy of what is referred to by the terms in the proposition, or it can concern the meaning ascribed to what is referred to by it. The subject of a proposition can be either a selective or a cyrioid (CP 8.181). Selectives are what are generally called quantifiers (cf. CP 5.450) and are subdivided into universal (all, any, no, etc.) and particular (some, at least one, etc.). Selectives are more or less "direction for finding an object" of the proposition (CP 8.181). Universal quantities are general because, when uttered, they invite the interpreter to pick any individual of the type named: "All humans are mortal" suggests that if you select any human you please, then that human will be mortal. On the other hand, particular quantifiers are vague (CP 5.450), since the claim that "Some humans are wise" does not specify to the interpreter which humans in particular are to be selected. To use Peirce's example: "A man whom I could mention seems to be a little conceited," made in the context of a party, is vague because "the sugges-tion here is that the man in view is the person addressed; but the utterer does not authorize such an interpretation or any other application of what he says" (CP 5.447). "'A *certain* man' means that the determination which is left *uncertain* to the reader or auditor is, nevertheless, or once *was certain* either to the utterer or some other person" (CP 5.505n1) .

Cyrioids include proper names, demonstratives, personal and relative pronouns, abstract and common nouns. Sometimes Peirce calls these singular quantities (CP 5.450). Again, their determination is set in the dialogic relation between speaker and auditor. A proper name, for example, "denotes a single individual well known to exist by the utterer and the interpreter" (CP 4.243). The reference of the proper name is fixed by the users of the name:

> Suppose, for example, two Englishmen to meet in a continental railway carriage. If one mentions Charles the Second, the other need not consider what possible Charles the Second is meant. It is no doubt the English Charles Second. Charles the Second of England was quite a different man on different days, and it might be said that without further specification the subject is not identified. But the two Englishmen have no purpose in splitting hairs in their talk. . . . (CP 5.448n1)

The reference of a proper name is fixed or made determinate relative to the universe of discourse or discourse community between utterer and interpreter: "It is useless to attempt to discuss the genuineness and possession of a personality beneath the histrionic presentation of Theodore Roosevelt with a person who recently has come from Mars and never heard of Theodore before" (CP 8.314).[26]

It seems, then, that proper names and other terms are determinate relative to a certain universe of discourse and a certain purpose among utterers and interpreters who share that discourse community.[27] As Peirce says, "we can only say, in a general way that a term, however determinate, may be more determinate still, but not that it can be absolutely determinate. Such a term as 'the Second Philip of Macedon' is still capable of logical division into Philip drunk and Philip sober, for example" (CP 3.93).

Similarly in regard to demonstratives. They can be made determinate relative to the shared universe of discourse or collateral experience of the speaker and utterer:

> Two men meet on a country road. One says to the other, "That house is on fire." "What house?" "Why, the house about a mile to my right." Let this speech be taken down and shown to anybody in the neighborhood village, and it will appear that the language by itself does not fix the house. But the person addressed sees where the speaker is standing, recognizes his *right* hand side (a word having a most singular mode of signification), estimates a line . . . and looking there, sees a house. It is not the language alone . . . but the language taken in connection with the auditor's own experiential associations of contiguity, which determines for him what house is meant. It is requisite then, in order to show what we are talking or writing about, to put the hearer's or reader's mind into real, active connection with the concatenation of experience or of fiction with

> which we are dealing, and, further, to draw his attention to, and identify, a certain number of particular points in such concatenation. (CP 3.419)

In regard to the common noun, its function

> is the same as that of the Proper Name. That is it merely draws attention to an object and so puts its interpreter into a condition to learn whatever there may be to be learned from such attention. Now attention can only be drawn to what is already in experience. A proper name can only function as such if the utterer and interpreter are already more or less familiar with the object it names. But the peculiarity of a common noun is that it undertakes to draw attention to an object with which the interpreter may have no acquaintance. For this purpose it calls up to his mind such an image as a verb calls up, appeals to his memory that he has seen different objects [as] the subjects of that image . . . and then of those which might be so recollected or imagined, the noun indefinitely names one. (MS 515: 23)

In this case the common noun is indeterminate because it is *general*.
Vagueness also applies to predicates; but whereas the vagueness of the subject of a proposition is due to the indefiniteness of reference, vagueness of the predicate is due to the indefiniteness of the *essential* depth of a term, i.e., its conceptual or conventional definition (cf. CP 2.410):

> We may use *indefiniteness in depth or vagueness* to denote any indefiniteness which primarily affects the essential depth of a sign, that is, the predicates or other consequences which its affirmation may by logical necessity carry with it, and which will, at least usually, thereby affect its logical breadth, or the total of subjects of which it can be affirmed in a given state of information. (MS 283: 321)

Peirce gives a good example of this type of vagueness:

> . . . the question whether a newly found skeleton was the skeleton of a man rather than of an anthropoid ape, the reply "yes and no" might, in a certain sense, be justifiable. Namely, owing to our conception of what a man is having been formed without thinking of the possibility of such a creature as that to which this skeleton belongs, the question really has no definite meaning (MS 596: 20).

Thus, due to the indefiniteness of the definition of "man," it is uncertain whether a skeleton which has some attributes not generally considered human should be called a human skeleton. Consider also the following example:

> What has been said of subjects (concerning vagueness) is as true of predicates. Suppose the chat of our pair of Englishmen had fallen upon the color of Charles II's hair. Now that colors are seen quite differently by different retinas is known. That the chromatic sense is indeed more varied than it is positively known to be is quite likely. It is very unlikely that either of the travellers is trained to observe colors or is a master of their nomenclature. But if one says that Charles II had dark auburn hair, the other will understand him quite precisely enough for all their purposes; and it will be a determinate predication. (CP 5.448n1)

In general, determination is established relative to a commens or universe of discourse and relative to the purposes of the communicators; absolute determination would be a determination for all possible universes of discourse or discourse communities.

So far we've examined relatively simple acts of communication, those which attempt to fix reference and establish meaning of basic terms. The matter becomes more difficult when more complex speech acts are involved. Consider for example, the case of assertion.[28] The study of assertion is a matter of universal rhetoric (CP 2.333). Anticipating speech-act theory, Peirce makes a distinction between the proposition, "which is the meaning of a sentence, and which remains the same in whatever language it is expressed," and "whether it is believed or doubted, asserted ... commanded ... or put as a question" (MS L75: 396). This corresponds to Austin's well-known distinction between the propositional content and the illocutionary act.[29] Thus, in making an assertion, there are at least two levels of communication to consider: on the one hand, there is the communication of the propositional content ("it is cold today"), and on the other, there is the communication between utterer and interpreter in the context of that propositional content (I'm asserting that it is cold today).

On the first level, the utterer wants the interpreter to understand (in the sense of intelligibility) *what* is being asserted. This involves all the matters discussed so far, namely, fixing the reference and general meaning of the terms employed in the proposition.

On the second level, assertion is not simply the communication of propositional content but is also concerned with other purposes the utterer might have; it involves an attempt to do something with that propositional content to some interpreter other than just understanding it: to get the interpreter to believe what is asserted, to create what Austin called the perlocutionary effect. The effectual interpretant, in this context, roughly corresponds to the perlocutionary effect (assuming that it is successful). It is what is achieved in the interpreter by means of the communication. The propositional content has established in the utterer an intentional interpretant, manifested as the intention to convey not only the belief in the proposition but thereby also a willingness to justify that belief. Although belief in a proposition is the willingness to act upon it, it is also the willingness to assert it: "assertion consists in the furnishing of evidence by the speaker to the listener that the speaker believes something, that is, finds a certain idea to be definitely compulsory on a certain occasion" (CP 2.335). In this context Peirce speaks about the responsibility of the assertor for the assertion:

> an assertion belongs to the class of phenomena like going before a notary and making an affidavit, executing a deed, signing a note, of which the essence is that one voluntarily puts oneself into a situation in which penalties will be incurred unless some proposition is true. (CP 8.313)

The cominterpretant, in this context, is the mutual effect from the process of communication. The effectual interpretant may or may not establish in the interpreter a belief concerning the proposition that was communicated, but the cominterpretant creates in both utterer and interpreter a certain connection not present prior to the communication: first, a certain mutual understanding of what is happening (an assertion is being made) and a mutual understanding of its effects. Each understands that the goal of the communication is to convey to the interpreter the utterer's conviction that the propositional content is true; that the interpreter has a right to demand proof or justification for not only the sincerity of the conviction, but the truth of the proposition; conversely, the utterer must be prepared to supply such proofs;[30] and if these ideas are performed successfully, the utterer believes that the interpreter now believes what the utterer believes, and the interpreter believes similarly.

Universal Rhetoric as a Study of the Formal Conditions of Inquiry

The significance of a sign is represented in its growth and development; inquiry is one of the principal means by which signs evolve within a human community. Consequently, universal rhetoric in this regard would be a study of the process of inquiry (MS L75: 1) and the nature of communities which best promote such inquiry.

As previously argued, the leading principles of the three fundamental forms of reasoning, abduction, deduction, and induction, lead to the conclusion that truth is the accomplishment of *inquiry*, understood as a process of the application of these patterns of reasoning by a community of inquirers; and as mentioned many times, this "social principle" (the need to appeal to a community) is rooted intrinsically in logic (CP 5.354). Logic suggests a connection with community, since it is only in the community of inquirers that logical thinking can be constituted (CP 2.654). There is consequently an inherent connection of logic to inquiry and inquiry to community, and universal rhetoric is concerned primarily with the question of inquiry in the context of community. Inquiry, as opposed to simple inferencing, is a *practice*, a "mode of life" (CP 7.54): "if I am asked to what the wonderful success of modern sciences is due, I shall suggest that to gain the secret of that, it is necessary to consider science as living and therefore not as knowledge already acquired but as the concrete life of the men who are working to find out the truth" (CP 7.50).

A practice involves a relatively settled set of habits, dispositions, conventions, and rules, that is, a set of final and ultimate interpretants which determine (in the sense of constrain rather than control) its practitioners toward a certain kind of action (cf. CP 5.487 ff.). Practices are sustained within a community. Clearly, depending on the constitution of the community, some practices will be favored and sustained over others; this is certainly true of inquiry practices. Thus, in regard to the question of inquiry, universal rhetoric should address not only the question of best method (hence universal rhetoric understood as methodeutic becomes clearer) but also the issue of the best community which would sustain the best method. Part of the job of universal rhetoric is to determine the conditions under which a community could engage in and sustain the best method of inquiry.

Methods of Settling Opinion

The primary purpose of inquiry is the settlement of opinion, the fixation of belief (CP 5.377), the achievement of genuine consensus. According to Peirce, there are five general methods of settling opinion or fixing belief: the method of tenacity, authority, the a priori method, the method of public opinion, the method of investigation or inquiry (CP 5.377–5.385, 7.317–7.318).

The method of tenacity employs simply the will to believe something true without entertaining any belief or evidence contrary to it (cf. CP 5.377). Generally it seeks to affirm beliefs that are held by habit or custom which, for various reasons, suit a person comfortably. To the extent that there is an investment in the belief, there is a resistance to modifying or questioning that belief. Peirce seems to suggest that it is a method employed primarily by individuals (CP 5.377), but there is no reason why it couldn't also apply to groups or communities which hold a set of beliefs homogeneously.

It is clear that in order for this method to work, it must be successful at isolating and insulating the individual or community from conflicting beliefs. But this, according to Peirce, is precisely the weakness of the method (CP 5.378). This may work to some extent in communities that are geographically isolated from others, are homogeneous, and are successful in eliminating contrary opinions from public discourse, but this is much more difficult in heterogeneous and diverse cultures where communication links are well-established. Exposure to contrary opinions and beliefs is inevitable, so that radical attempts to insulate individuals in this context can only lead to rather extreme forms of suppression (cf. CP 5.378).

The method of authority seeks to establish beliefs by the imposition on the general population of beliefs held by those in some position of power over that population (cf. CP 5.379), and history has shown it to be the chief means by which beliefs are fixed (CP 5.379). The beliefs that are espoused are usually those that are beneficial to the authority, since they have a tendency, if followed, to maintain that authority (cf. CP 5.379, 7.317). To maintain authority, it must employ techniques of isolation and insulation inherent in the method of tenacity. However, since it is an imposition of the will on others, as opposed to the fiat of the will in the method of tenacity (CP 5.382), it often engages in extremely cruel or barbarous methods in that regard (CP 5.379). The method of tenacity seems to be employed out of an internal motivation to retain beliefs that one wants to retain for various reasons such as security, familiarity, or comfortableness; but in the method of authority, as Peirce characterizes it, one retains these beliefs out of fear, resulting from the effort by the authority to control the beliefs in the community.

But this is precisely the weakness of this method of fixing belief. It must impose total control over the lives of the members of its community, and this is nearly impossible, since opinions, beliefs, norms, and ideas contrary to the ones enforced will inevitably infiltrate the community (CP 5.382). Once such contrariness is introduced, especially if such ideas will benefit those most oppressed in the community, a crack in the power of authority develops which requires authority to either respond more harshly to the rebelliousness or to open up the avenues of power to more people; in the first case, severe oppression will lead to revolt, and in the second case, existing authority will eventually be usurped.

In this last case, authority must give way to the method of public opinion. In this method, the fixing of belief is established not by imposing a set of beliefs on members of a community but by getting them to enthusiastically adopt a set of beliefs of their own accord. Under this method it is still possible to control the community's beliefs, but it must be done in a way that appeals to the population other than through force or intimidation, that is, out of self-interest or commonly held sentiments, fears, or hatreds (cf. CP 7.324). But this turns out to be a rather unstable basis of establishing belief, precisely because the appeal is to sentiments, appearances, and opinions that are not firmly established. This method has a tendency to create sweeping and rapid changes but ones that do not persist as circumstances or public mood changes (cf. CP 7.318).

Another method of fixing belief is what Peirce calls the a priori method, a method that establishes beliefs on the basis of what is agreeable to reason (CP 5.382). Rather than an appeal to authority or to popular public sentiment, the attempt here is to establish a universal set of fundamental beliefs, independent of any community but based on what is, nonetheless, common to any member of any community—the capacity to reason. It is an attempt to deliver belief from capriciousness and accident (CP 5.383). Reason alone can establish fundamental criteria by which the justification of certain beliefs or the adjudication among conflicting beliefs can be established. But as an analysis of the practitioners of this method shows (Descartes, Kant, Hegel, and the classical metaphysicians would be examples [CP 5.382n1]), the method is really an intellectual analogue to the method of authority and tenacity (CP 5.383), since it involves simply an attempt to justify what one is inclined to think (CP 5.382n1). Usually it takes what is common in the culture, such as the belief in the existence of God, and makes it out to be a proposition self-evident to reason, elevating its status to something that is universal or necessary (cf. CP 5.382n1). It seems simply to be a means of ascribing additional justification to something that is well accepted by the community to which the inquirer belongs.

The weakness of the method lies in the fact that the claim of self-evidence, necessity, or universality is always mediated through the reasoner and depends, to some degree, on the reasoner's cognitive or psychological ability to intuit or see clearly and distinctly that the belief is a universal or necessary belief. Consequently different reasoners will intuit different universals, and the history of metaphysics shows not a progress in the matters of metaphysics but more often an alternation and variety of views. If two intuitions conflict, there is no further basis of appeal by which to adjudicate between the proposed universals; if there is no preexisting consensus concerning the universals, such a consensus cannot be achieved by the a priori method alone.

It should not be thought, however, that these various methods of settling opinion are without advantage. The strength of the method of tenacity lies in its simplicity and directness (CP 5.386). Persons who pursue it are "distinguished for their decision of character; they do not waste time trying to make up their minds what they want, but, fastening like lightning upon whatever alternative comes first, they hold to it to the end, whatever happens, without an instant's irresolution. This is one of the splendid qualities which generally accompany brilliant, unlasting success. It is impossible not to envy the men who can dismiss reason, although we know how it must turn out at last" (CP 5.386).

The a priori method allows a certain comfortableness and security that is less likely with the method of inquiry. It assures us of the foundations of our thought, since it supposes that they cannot be otherwise, given their intuitive and a priori character, although that security may be questioned in the long run (CP 5.386). The method of inquiry, on the other hand, allows that foundational principles are also subject to investigation, since they are fallible and subject to genuine doubt.

The method of authority "will always govern the mass of mankind" (CP 5.386); it is a deeply ingrained approach to settling opinion. Its advantage is that it can more directly establish peace (CP 5.386), since it either eliminates or controls any opposition to its position by suppression or force.

Although these methods vary in the degree of success in fixing belief, they all fail, according to Peirce, in establishing belief in the long run. Critical logic has argued that true belief can be established by means of an ongoing process of inquiry, guided by the leading principles of abduction, deduction, and induction. These engender certain practical postulates or presuppositions which must be realized in a community of a certain sort in order to be ultimately successful. These presuppositions can be seen as more formalized expressions of the logical sentiments at the basis of genuine community; and it is these presuppositions which the other methods of fixing belief lack. These are the possibility of truth, the likelihood of error, and the continuity of growth. The first is supported by the metaphysics of realism, the second by the doctrine of fallibilism, and the third by the principle of synechism. The possibility of truth rests on an appeal to the real, understood as something that cannot be changed by human convention (although it can be conventionally expressed), but which, on the other hand, unceasingly tends to influence thought (CP 5.384, 5.384n1). This is the essential core of realism. But it must also be realized that the methods of inquiry are eminently fallible given the very nature of reasoning, especially abduction and induction (CP 1.141): "on the whole, then, we cannot in any way reach perfect certitude nor exactitude. We never can be absolutely sure of anything, nor can we with any probability ascertain the exact value of any measure or general ratio" (CP 1.147). Fallibilism serves as the expression of the presupposition that all our beliefs are subject to error. The doctrine of fallibilism, however, fits within the general idea of synechism, that inquiry grows, expands, and diversifies (CP 1.171). Thus the presupposition of growth of information rests on the background of synechistic community. It is only the method of inquiry or science that embraces all these practical postulates fully (cf. CP 5.384). Each of the other methods violates the presuppositions in one way or another. None of the other methods admits the possibility of error in regard to authority, dogmatic belief, or a priori foundations; and each relies on some expression of human convention as the ultimate source of justification (even in the case of religious authority, it is still humanly interpreted and, consequently, fallible [CP 1.143]). In the long run, then, these methods will not succeed in fixing belief.

The method of inquiry, given the way it is, does not incur the advantages of the other methods except in the long run. Unlike the method of tenacity, it does not yield strength, simplicity, or directness of beliefs; there is more of a tentativeness to beliefs until they are secured by further inquiry. The method of inquiry does not yield security of beliefs, since their foundations may be subject to genuine doubt. The method of inquiry does not secure peace, since it allows opposition to existing beliefs. Yet because these methods cannot maintain their advantages over the long run, from the perspective of future welfare, these advantages should be sacrificed in favor of the method of inquiry. This requires the willingness to forgo immediate for long-run advantage (CP 5.387).

The Community of Inquiry

The *method* of inquiry contains practical presuppositions which engender a certain *community* of inquiry. We can discern the character of this community on the basis of those presuppositions. In general, the community of inquiry would, first, encourage self-criticism, that is, encourage reflection on the beliefs presently held (as opposed to a community bent on tenacity), but only if such reflection is warranted by genuine doubt (as opposed to the artificial doubt of Descartes). Second, the community of inquiry would allow and encourage openness toward criticism (as opposed to tenacious and authoritative communities). Participants in inquiry would be allowed the opportunity to criticize, to refute, as well as present alternative views.[31] Arbitrary exclusion from this process would be incomprehensible under this view.[32] Third, the community of inquiry must encourage a healthy skepticism (as opposed to the dogmatic community), such that any belief, in principle, is subject to criticism (provided there are genuine reasons for doubt). Fourth, such a community could not employ force or coercion in the attempt to reach consensus (as opposed to communities based on authority).[33] Fifth, the community would employ criteria and evidence that had a public quality to it and a universal appeal,[34] criteria that were not clearly constituted by the opinion of some segment of the community; that is, the criteria are not dependent on the opinions of those in a hierarchy but must be publicly accepted. Finally, the community would use universal consensus as the *measure* of the truth of a belief.

This community is contrasted to an authority-based community, which would see the ultimate justification of beliefs in the pronouncements of superior individuals or institutions which hold the highest position in the social hierarchy. A tenacious community must establish elaborate means to censor outside information; and similarly, a dogmatic community must also provide mechanisms which will prevent the questioning of its fundamental or revered beliefs.

The Teleology of Sign Development and the Growth of Concrete Reasonableness

Given the character of the community of inquiry, universal rhetoric is still concerned to articulate its purposes, goals, and ends. Peirce suggests that part of universal rhetoric is concerned with a general doctrine of "methods of attaining purposes" (CP 2.108). In a community of inquiry the growth of information will have a certain effect on sign agencies connected to the system. As the state of information grows closer to an exact expression of the real, this would lead to habits of sign interpretation that would guarantee, as far as possible, correct comportment toward the world and other sign agencies who inhabit it. In that case, the community of inquiry grows toward what Peirce calls "concrete reasonableness" (CP 5.3, CP 5.433)

If universal rhetoric is understood as a concern with "methods of attaining purposes," this in turn "should spring from a still more general doctrine of the nature of teleological action . . . " (CP 2.108). This makes sense, since growth, change, and development are inherent in the very character of sign and inquiry; the triadic character of the sign, as we have seen, lends itself to teleological and intentional analysis ("a symbol is essentially a purpose" [NEM 4: 243]).[35] Understanding how the community of inquiry attains the goal of concrete reasonableness relies on an accurate understanding of teleological action.

Aristotle' s account of causation served as a model for explaining why something is or why something happens for generations of philosophers and scientists.[36] This is to be accounted by reference to four possible causes: formal, material, efficient, and final. For example, "why this house?" In one sense the answer is found in its formal cause, in this case, the blueprints as expression of the general idea of the house; in one sense it is the material cause, the wood and nails and bricks out of which it is built; in another sense it is the fact that the carpenter, bricklayers, electricians, and others used applied techniques to the materials in accordance with the blueprints for the house (the efficient cause); but also it is there because someone desired to live in a house just like this one (the final cause). Beginning with Galileo, much of modern science eschewed the idea of final causes in favor of studying mostly efficient causes, that is, the mechanisms and forces involved in motion, rather than any larger picture concerning the "why" of that motion.[37] Typically such questions led to metaphysical or religious speculation that was not observable or confirmable by experiment and was, in any case, thought to be irrelevant to the purpose of science.

Contrary to this trend in modern science, Peirce viewed questions of teleology and final causes as a serious matter for inquiry. Part of this was due to the influence of the theory of evolution, which seemed to demand some explanation of constrained growth and development. However, in this matter of teleology, although Peirce adopted many of the ideas of Aristotle, he was led in many ways to a different conception of final cause.[38] Aristotle sees ultimate final causes as perfected processes (e.g., happiness in the sphere of human action or the unmoved mover in cosmic motion); these processes assert an influence over imperfect processes, which are moved to emulate them. Thus the sense of final cause is, first, bound up with the notion of perfection and goodness of the process, but, second, suggests that the final cause is, in some sense, prior to that which it influences. On the other hand, Peirce seems to have a less valuative and more mathematical notion of final cause, but argues for a then relatively novel claim that final causes, or ultimate order, emerge rather than existing prior to the phenomena they order, more specifically that order evolves out of chance or chaos (cf. CP 6.33)—not unlike the general conceptions of Ilya Prigogine.[39] This view is contrary to the more traditional view of a final cause as something that preexists and constrains unordered phenomena in a certain direction). What we discover instead are patterns that emerge in the process of evolution which then are successful at maintaining and reproducing themselves, so to speak.[40]

To distinguish this sense of teleology from Aristotle's perfective sense, we might, along with Peirce, call such processes *finious*, which is simply the sense that things have a tendency to move toward a final state (CP 7.471), a state of generalizable character (CP 1.211). Peirce uses the example of the diffusion of gases to illustrate his idea (NEM 4: 66).[41] The random motions of the gas molecules tend irreversibly toward the result that the gas is uniformly distributed, and this will result regardless of the particular motions (or forces) within the system. It is in this sense that Peirce argued that "chance begets order" (CP 6.297; cf. CP 7.471).

The same sort of analysis is applied by Peirce to Darwin's theory of evolution, which he sees, in a sense, as an application of the theory of gases to biology (CP 5.364). In evolution, fortuitous variation and selection act to create a certain self-sustaining order (CP 6.296), that is, species that are able—due precisely to their variation—to survive, to maintain themselves within a certain environment. Evolution does not destine certain species to develop but simply results in the more tautologous generalization that those species that are present are present because their variations allow them to survive in that environment.[42]

The most essential character of finious processes becomes clearer through these examples, namely, that such processes are *corrective* processes. The corrective character is expressed by the selection and variation that goes on in such processes,[43] although such corrective processes have a statistical or mathematical character to them. In a certain sense the motions of gas molecules are corrected until they reach the point of uniform distribution; similarly, variation and selection allow species to be corrected toward the norm of survival within a certain environment; ants will correct their movements—when faced with an obstacle—in order to reach a food source; human beings will correct their behavior in order to attain certain goals. It is precisely because the cosmos exhibits such corrective processes at all levels—although in various gradations—that Peirce supposes a continuity between human mental processes and other types of processes, since the hallmark of mentality is correction (CP 1.269, 6.101, 6.24 ff.). But human mental processes are capable of *self-correction* or self-control (CP 5.418),[44] that is, intentional or deliberate selection and variation (CP 5.442). As Peirce writes, "in its higher stages, evolution takes place more and more largely through self-control . . . " (CP 5.433; cf. CP 5.33, 1.573, 1.591–1.607, 5.417–5.421; MS 477: 19). Self-correction and self-control are the essence of reasoning (CP 5.108), and reasoning is best expressed through the process of inquiry.

In the process of inquiry, then, we find the highest expression of finious processes. For in such processes we find the movement toward the determination of signs, the interpretation of signs, whose effects create in us certain habits of interpretation and action, habits which culminate in a general "concrete reasonableness" (CP 5.3, 5.433) as inquiry moves toward consensus. "The whole purpose of a sign is that it should be interpreted in another sign and its whole purpose lies in the special character which it imparts to that interpretant. When a sign determines an interpretant of itself in another sign, it produces an effect external to itself" (CP 8.191). But this is not to suggest that the process of interpretation is a free-for-all, an interpretation for the sake of interpretation, an indefinite variation of interpretation; rather, the goal of inquiry, of logic, is to determine which of the possible interpretations of signs are truly adapted to be the proper development of that sign (CP 4.9), and so the full employment of semeiotic—grammar, critical logic, and universal rhetoric—is needed to guide finious processes in the proper direction:

> The meaning of a proposition is itself a proposition. Indeed, it is no other than the very proposition of which it is the meaning: it is a translation of it. But of the myriads of forms into which a proposition may be translated, what is that one which is to be called its very meaning? It is, according to the pragmaticist, that form in which the proposition becomes applicable to human conduct . . . that form which is most directly applicable to self-control. . . . (CP 5.427)

In a clarification of pragmaticism, Peirce makes it clear that "the meaning of a concept" lies in the way in which individual reaction "contributes" to the development of "concrete reasonableness" (CP 5.3). "The *summum bonum*," according to the pragmaticist, "does not consist in action, but makes it consist in that process of evolution whereby the existent comes more and more to embody those generals which were . . . said to be *destined*, which is what we strive to express in calling them *reasonable*. In its higher stages, evolution takes place more and more largely through self-control . . . " (CP 5.433). Synechism is "founded on the notion that the coalescence, the becoming continuous, the becoming governed by laws . . . are but phases of one and the same process of the growth of reasonableness" (CP 5.4).

Concrete reasonableness is an end-in-itself and so inherently admirable (CP 1.615). Ultimately the characterization of its admirableness is informed by aesthetics, the study of ends (CP 1.612). It cannot be justified by something other than itself, since all attempts at justification must appeal to reason. And so it has a quality not unlike Aristotle's notion of happiness: it is an end which by the force of its own being serves to ground all things and move semeiosis in a certain direction.

NOTES

Preface

1. Letter to Cassius Keyser, April 10, 1908. Cited in Brent (1993: 43).

1. The Discipline of Semeiotic

1. For a detailed analysis of the evolution of Peirce's classification of the sciences and the role of logic, but also the philosophical problems associated with it, see Kent (1987).

2. For a justification of this, see CP 3.429, where mathematics is called diagrammatic or iconic thinking; there is a claim made that logic employs a similar form of observation: "Logical truth is grounded on a sort of observation of the same kind as that upon which mathematics is grounded" (MS 293: 14). For a more detailed examination of Peirce's view of mathematical reasoning, see Murphey (1961) and chapter 3 in this volume.

3. Peirce suggests that these two subclasses are distinct, in the sense that although they have some influence on one another, in the end physics does not supply principles to psychics (CP 1.255). This statement argues against the thesis of reductionism; that is confirmed by Peirce's insistence on the distinction between efficient causes (as the domain of physical sciences) and final causes as the domain of the psychical ones (cf. CP 1.257). For a discussion of how the notion of final causes serves to classify the sciences, see Kent (1987: 88–89); see also Pape (1993).

4. Peirce writes that "this classification [of the sciences] . . . borrows its idea from Comte's classification; namely, the idea that one science depends upon another for fundamental principles, but does not furnish such principles to that other" (CP 1.180; cf. CP 1.238).

5. For an account of the influence of the classical trivium of grammar, logic, and rhetoric, see Perreiah (1989), Michael (1977), and Savan (1988). Fisch (1978) recognized five versions of this division in Peirce's thought:

Spring 1865: Universal Grammar, Logic, Universal Rhetoric
May 1865: General Grammar, General Logic, General Rhetoric
1867: Formal Grammar, Logic, Formal Rhetoric
1897: Pure Grammar, Logic Proper, Pure Rhetoric
1903: Speculative Grammar, Critic, and Methodeutic

However, these appear to be basically the same but with different terminology. In this book, I have adopted the following terminology for this division: semeiotic grammar, critical logic, universal rhetoric.

6. "*Pragmatics* is that portion of semiotic which deals with the origin, uses and effects of signs within the behavior in which they occur; *semantics* deals with the signification of signs in all modes of signifying; *syntactics* deals with the combination of signs without regard for their specific significations or their relation to the behavior in which they occur" (Morris 1946: 219; cf. R. Carnap 1942: 9).

7. According to Peirce, all propositions have a subject and predicate (CP 2.316, 5.553).

8. There are certainly other important differences between semeiotic and semiology understood as a *theory*. Here I am focusing on the difference in the character of semeiotic and semiology as *disciplines*. According to most commentators on this matter (Deledalle 1967a, 1967b; Stetter 1979), the most important difference between Saussure's theory and Peirce's is the difference between the dyadic and triadic concept of the sign, and especially Peirce's notion of the interpretant. But see Liszka (1993) for an account which suggests that Saussure's notion of value can be considered to be the conceptual equivalent of the interpretant.

9. Most of the major French thinkers responsible for movements such as phenomenology, structuralism, deconstruction, and postmodernism were influenced by Saussure. For example, Lévi-Strauss mostly adopted the framework of Saussure, despite the enthusiasm of his linguistic mentor, Roman Jakobson, for Peirce. There are a few mentions of Peirce in Lévi-Strauss's corpus (see 1968) which show a passing acquaintance with the American thinker, but his theory is primarily Saussurean. The French phenomenologist Merleau-Ponty (1964), when he does reflect on the nature of signs, uses the voice of Saussure. Barthes (1967) saw semiology as practically synonymous with the name of Saussure. The early Lacan (1957) used Saussure's concept of the sign as the basis for his psychoanalytical theory. Baudrillard (1981) constructs his "political economy" of the sign primarily on Saussure's concept of the sign. Of course, although Derrida (1978) allies himself with a Peirce of his own invention, still grammatology is built out of a reflection on Saussure.

10. See Guiraud (1975) and Hawkes (1977: 24).

11. See Mill (1979: 421).

2. Semeiotic Grammar

1. I prefer the use of *sign* to *representamen*, although Peirce does make a distinction between the two. Benedict (1985) traces the history of the term "representamen." According to Benedict, Peirce uses this term occasionally prior to 1903, and in 1903 does use it more frequently than at any other time (CP 2.233 ff.), but then drops it from use after 1903 (cf. MS L463: 60–63). The distinction between sign and representamen is not entirely clear (cf. CP 1.540, 4.447) but seems to be based on the distinction between our "familiar" or

"commonsense" notion of "sign" and the more formal or essential character of the sign. Thus Peirce writes, "The concrete subject that represents I call a sign or a representamen. I use the two words, *sign* and *representamen*, differently. By a *sign* I mean anything which conveys any definite notion of an object in any way, as such conveyers of thought are familiarly known to us. Now I start with this familiar idea and make the best analysis I can of what is essential to a sign, and I define a *representamen* as being whatever that analysis applies to" (CP 1.540; cf. Savan 1988: 15 and Short 1981: 198). However, in this same passage he also seems to indicate that the term "representamen" has wider application than "sign," the latter restricted to human minds, while the former need not make such a reference (cf. Savan 1988: 16 and Short 1981: 198). If that is the essence of the distinction between the two terms, then the term "quasi-sign," which Peirce uses later on in 1906, might have the same sense as representamen (cf. CP 5.473, 4.550–551). But in any case, whatever the distinction, Peirce apparently no longer saw any use for the term "representamen." However, Benedict wants to reinstitute it as a substitute for the word "sign" when what is referred to by that term is the correlate associated with "object" and "interpretant"; the word "sign" can be reserved, then, as the name for the triadic relation among "representamen," "object," "interpretant" (1985: 266). Although this may be of some terminological convenience, it doesn't seem to have much textual support. It's probably better, then, to heed Peirce's wishes and drop the term from usage (cf. Short 1981: 198), although Savan (1986: 139) still saw a useful purpose to the distinction.

2. The claim that for Peirce all signs involve an object is supported by most Peirce scholars, although how they interpret this claim varies, as we will see shortly. Ransdell (1976: 101–106) argues that for Peirce "the object is essential in all semiosis." Similarly, Pape (1991: 145) says that for Peirce the "object" is an "essential ingredient" of a sign. This interpretation is also held by Short (1981: 217), Houser (1992: xxxix), and Savan (1988: 25, 1994: 189). Greenlee (1973: 23, 111) may be the exception in this regard. But as Ransdell (1976: 106) notes, "Greenlee's proposal to eliminate reference to the object as generic to the sign-relation is . . . misguided *as* an interpretational revision of Peirce, whatever independent merit it may have."

In addition to the question of interpretation, some scholars of Peirce, however, criticize this claim. Greenlee (1973: 58–59) does so, as mentioned. But this is also the opinion of Singer (1983). She argues that "not every sign is a 'sign of'. . . " (1987: 95). Her examples include grammatical connectives, imperative commands, and musical notes. Short (1981: 217), Savan (1988: 25; 1994: 189), and Ransdell (1976: 105) claim that these and other examples are not real concerns, mostly because Peirce's sense of object is more comprehensive than most theories, so that it can include physical things, as well as abstractions, relations, fictions, laws, etc. So "and" may simply represent the abstract relation of conjunction (see Savan 1994: 189). Also there is the consideration that the object of a sign might be vague. For example, it's not entirely clear what the smell in the air of an autumn walk in the forest refers to, except to say, vaguely, that it represents the forest as such, in that regard. A musical note might simply act as an index, and so in a trivial sense represent the fact that it was produced by someone blowing a horn. But within the context of a musical piece, it is essentially vague, until its connection with other notes takes on a certain order so that it might begin to represent more clearly an aspect of a feeling which the composer wishes to produce in his audience. After all, it's quite possible that a sound is not a sign if it doesn't represent anything, although it is at least always an index of that which produces it.

Peirce's thesis, that all signs represent an object, has collateral support from the thesis of intentionality. For this reason it is tempting to compare the second formal condition with that theory. Searle, one of the more contemporary proponents of the theory, defines intentionality as that property of mental states (among which we assume mental signs) and events "by which they are directed at or about objects and states of affairs in the world" (1988: 1). An intentional state ("I believe it is raining") is composed of a representational content ("it is raining") and a certain psychological mode ("I believe") (1988: 11). Searle claims that the intentional object is just an object like any other; it is what some intentional state is about (1988: 16).

The difficulty with the intentionality thesis is that if mental states must be about something, then it would appear that there can be no mental states about fictional, false, or nonexistent things—which is clearly absurd. The more classical solutions, as found in early Brentano (1973), have involved a questionable ontology. Searle's solution seeks to avoid such ontological complexities. In cases of intentional states, such as "I believe the present king of France is bald," Searle argues that there is still a representational content ("the present king of France is bald"), but there is a failure of the representational content to refer to any intentional object. The intentional state is still about the king of France, but in this case there is no ordinary intentional object which it is about (1988: 17). This seems to be somewhat similar to Casteneda's account (1989) of proper names, where a proper name at least refers to its "internal object," understood as the general sense of its use within a language community. Thus the internal object of the "present king of France" is the sense of any proper name, namely, that there is only one individual called the king of France and, that all co-contextual uses of this name refer to the same male individual person. Grasping this internal object of "present king of France" has nothing to do with either knowing that such a person exists, or knowing how to locate this person, or even knowing that the name is intended to refer to an actual person (see Pape 1991: 143f.). In the case of fictional discourse, Searle says that

> we have a series of pretended speech acts, usually pretended assertives, and the fact that the speech act is only pretended breaks the word-to-world commitments of the normal assertive . . . in imagination the agent has a series of representations, but the mind-to-world direction of fit is broken by the fact that the representative contents are not contents of beliefs but are simply entertained . . . commitments to the conditions of satisfaction are deliberately suspended. (1988: 18)

Thus, for Searle, all signs may refer but not refer successfully, or they may pretend to refer.

Peirce appears to argue something similar: "every symbol, whether true or not, asserts itself to be applicable to some real thing" (W 1: 286–287). "Every symbol must have denotation that is must *imply* [italics added] the existence of some thing to which it is applicable" (W 1: 287). This is true even for fictional signs: "It may be a mere fiction; we may know it to be fiction; it may be intended to be a fiction. . . . In these cases, we pretend that we hold *realistic* opinions for the sake of indicating that our propositions are meant to be explicatory or analytic. But the symbol itself always pretends to be a true symbol and hence implies a reference to real things" (W 1: 287). Peirce writes: " . . . an apprehension . . . of the Object strictly so-called . . . is the 'immediate object' of the sign in the intention of the utterer. It may be that there is no such thing or fact in existence, or in any other mode of reality; but we surely shall not deny to the common picture of a phoenix or to a figure in naked truth in her well the name of a 'sign,' simply because the bird is a fiction and Truth an ens rationis . . . " (MS 318: 40–41).

Savan seems to agree with this interpretation: "Only some signs in special circumstances *refer* to anything" (1994: 188), but there is a subtlety with this view. He suggests that not all signs refer as opposed to saying that not all signs refer successfully. Savan wants to restrict reference to a property of certain linguistic signs; natural indices, such as thunder for rain and smoke for fire, do not refer to their objects (1994: 187). Peirce says in at least one place (W 1: 287) that every *symbol* must have denotation (even if it purports denotation); and in the main expression of his semeiotic theory, he does emphasize that every sign represents some object (CP 2.230). It could be that there is a difference between representation and denotation or reference. Peirce says that in regard to a symbol, it denotes its objects by means of its indices but represents it by means of its icon (cf. CP 2.295), implying that icons represent their objects, while indices can only denote their objects. But this view is not entirely consistent in Peirce, and it would suggest that if all signs represent, then it cannot be restricted simply to icons. Moreover, as opposed to Savan's interpretation, the proposed representation/denotation distinction would still suggest that a natural index such as smoke for fire would still denote fire, although it would not represent fire. This distinction would also be contrary to Goodman's view (1968: 5) that an icon, such as a picture, must denote in order to represent. If one wants to make a further refinement between reference, as pertaining to the intentionality of linguistic signs only, and denotation, as the name for the intentionality of all nonlinguistic signs, whatever other merits it might have, there is probably not much textual support for it in Peirce. I think we have to assume that by "representation" Peirce meant in a very general sense a directedness toward objects.

Another solution to this thorny problem of how every sign has an object yet some objects do not have actual existence is given by Ransdell. He argues (1976: 105) that although "the object is essential in all semiosis," it may only be the immediate object that is essential, since in fictive semiosis the "real" object (that is what I assume he means by the "dynamic object") is of no concern. The solution, as Ransdell interprets it, then, is that all signs have intentionality in the sense of immediate objects, but some (fictive signs) do not have dynamic objects. (See also Short [1981: 217]: "each sign, to be a sign, has at least an immediate object.") Pape (1991) argues similarly, although he employs Casteneda's theory of proper names to this end. Proper names that do not refer successfully still refer to an internal object, that is, the equivalent of Peirce's immediate object.

But if the interpretation that the dynamic object can also be fictive or imaginary (as Peirce implies [CP 8.314], and see n. 8; Short [1981: 217] also hints that the sign of a unicorn can have a dynamic object), then Ransdell's and Pape's solution would be suspect; every sign would also have to have a dynamic object as well; if there is anything about reality that it would convey, that would be determined through further interpretation of the sign. The dynamic object is not the goal of semeiosis but rather its initial determination. Information about the real is discovered in the endpoints of semeiosis. This suggests that an internally generated object (fictional or otherwise), even though not actually existing, can serve as a dynamic object, and even though it may not successfully refer to any existing thing, may still yield information about the real. This allows, on the one hand, mathematical constructs to express real relations (what Peirce calls the internally real—see n. 9) and, on the other hand, a play about Hamlet to say something truthful about human beings. The dynamic object plants the seed of determination in the sign, which upon further interpretation brings it in some cases to fruition, that is, some information about the real.

Short's solution (1981: 203–210) takes a different tack than either Ransdell's or Savan's. He wants to argue that the teleological character of semeiosis can account for intentionality (1981: 207); instead of articulating it in terms of a mental state, he would prefer to exteriorize it by accounting for it behaviorally, as the functional or goal-directed character of signs. For example, a noise can serve as a sign of a predator to a deer even if no such predator is there. The noise represents something that does not exist. But this breaks down to the following general form: an action, B (fleeing), is elicited by a sign-stimulus, A (the noise), as directed to a goal, C (safety from predators), only because the deer interprets the sign as a sign of predators (1981: 208). However, the danger in this interpretation is that it can easily lend itself to a behaviorist account. This suggests, more or less, that the deer is conditioned to respond to a certain sort of paired stimulus. If we follow Short's logic here, Pavlov's classical conditioning would be a model of intentionality. A reinforcer (food) is paired with a stimulus (a bell), so that even in the absence of food, the ringing of the bell would produce salivation. Short's example in this regard is striking: a dog runs from its cruel master upon seeing him raise the stick, even though there is no beating (1981: 208). The dog, already beaten several times, pairs the stick with the pain and so flees. Short wants to argue instead that this is goal-directed behavior made possible by the dog's interpretation of the raised stick as a sign of an impending beating. But the way it is framed makes it very conducive to a behaviorist analysis; behaviorists typically avoid teleological analysis in favor of dyadic, causal ones. Of course, a behaviorist reading of Peirce has been developed by Charles Morris. One wants to agree with Short that before a sign agency can respond to a stimulus, it must interpret the stimulus as a sign of some object, that is, it must involve a non-behavioral interpretation of the stimulus. Behaviorists would like to avoid the "black-box" of mental life, and completely exteriorize mentality in terms of stimulus-response patterns. But a good argument can be made that both classical and operant conditioning presuppose sign-interpreting agencies in some sense of the term. However, to explain semeiosis in terms of an exteriorized functional-behavioral or goal-directed response seems to defeat the precedence of semeiosis over conditioned response. Intentionality understood as an "interior" state is precisely the weapon which Searle uses to attack both behaviorism and functionalism. If one wishes to exteriorize intentionality then a behaviorist interpretation seems to be the most appropriate account of semeiosis. But just because intentionality is interiorized does not necessarily mean that the intentionality of signs is a subset of mentality or at least human mentality—which seems to be one of Short's concerns (1981: 203).

One plausible solution to this very difficult problem might be the following. Every sign is about a dynamic object *as* represented in the immediate object. However, if the dynamic object is not an actually existing thing, then reference in this strong, extensional sense (see Pape 1991: 147) will not be successful; that is, determinations of the sign which aim to locate its referent in the world of experience will not be successful; or, put differently, it will have no intentional objects in Searle's sense. Yet even if the dynamic object is not an actually existing thing (a completely determinate individual in Peirce's language; CP 6.349), then its function as a determinant of the sign process is not short-circuited. It is quite possible that something that is not externally existent but internally generated can still serve as a sign-determinant. The question of whether that determination is fruitful, in the sense of leading to some information about reality, is determined through its use in a process of inquiry.

If this interpretation has plausibility, then the idea that intentional objects are not always actually existing ones, or ordinary objects, is the point where Peirce and Searle part company. Although Peirce seems to agree with Searle's solutions to the intentionality paradoxes, and although there is some analytic agreement on the nature of intentionality ("representative content" = "immediate object" and "intentional object" = "dynamic object" in part), still Peirce disagrees with Searle on the ontological status of intentional objects. Searle only seems to allow intentional objects to be actually existing things in the perceived world; Peirce seems to allow objects of all phenomenological types to be intentional objects. How Peirce's ontology in this regard compares with Meinong's or Brentano's would be an interesting exploration, but not one appropriate for this note or even for this book, although some things can be said nonetheless. We know that the modern theory of intentionality has its roots in Franz Brentano and Edmund Husserl, both of whom were Peirce's contemporaries. I can find no evidence, however, that Peirce was familiar with either Brentano's or Husserl's theories of intentionality. He seemed unaware of Brentano, but was familiar with Husserl's work on logic in *Logische Untersuchungen* (CP 2.152, 4.7)—although he seemed unsettled by its propensity toward psychologism (CP 4.7).

They both use the term "phenomenology" but in much different senses (cf. Spiegelberg 1956).

Peirce does employ the notion of logical intention as derived from classic Scholastic sources (CP 3.94, 4.80), especially the work of Scotus as Peirce knew it (cf. McKeon 1952, Moore 1964). For Peirce, *second intentions* are the objects of understanding considered as representations, and the *first intentions* to which this applies are the objects of those representations (W 2: 56). This appears to be the basis of Peirce's distinction between *immediate* and *dynamic* objects and is similar to Searle's distinction between representational content and intentional object. The Scholastic source also seems to be the inspiration for Brentano's thesis of intentionality: "Every mental phenomena is characterized by what the Scholastics of the Middle Ages called the intentional (or mental) inexistence of an object, and what we might call . . . reference to a content, direction toward an object . . . or immanent objectivity" (1973: 88). In his early work, Brentano adopts an ontology that has notorious difficulties in dealing with intentional objects that have no actual existence, and therefore he drops it later on. Searle completely rejects, and does not even see a need for, the Meinong/Brentano ontology. It is clear that for Peirce there is a wide ontology of intentional objects, since the dynamic object is not restricted to just actually existing things but includes fictions and possibles. It would be very interesting to explore Peirce's ontology in this matter (as complex and somewhat inchoate as it is), but this might turn out to be a treatise in itself, so I hesitate to speculate about it here. For more discussion of Peirce's complex ontological distinctions, see n. 9.

3. There is a qualification to this rule. Some signs, such as indices (cf. CP 2.304) and icons (CP 2.247), are not *genuinely* triadic, according to Peirce; rather they are *degenerately* triadic, though triadic nonetheless (cf. CP 1.366–7). A symbol, such as THE, is genuinely triadic, because the *connection* or *relation* of the sign with its object is established by means of its (conventional) interpretation as representing that object. Without that interpretation it would have no connection or relation with that object (cf. CP 2.304, 2.247). On the other hand, an index has its *relation* or *connection* to its object independent of any interpretant which might interpret it as representing that object (cf. CP 2.304). Thus an animal track in the snow is the causal effect of that animal passing that way, and would have that connection regardless of any interpretant. However, in that case, the sign's ability to *represent* that object still requires an interpretant. So the formal requirement of triadicity is still in place even in the case of indices and icons. I think this solution to the anomaly is more consonant with Peirce's analysis and requires less conceptual manipulation than that found in Peterson (1983), who deals with this problem at length. His solution requires that we make a distinction between the essence of the sign and existence or actuality of a sign (1983: 27). The evidence he uses for that distinction (CP 2.247) is rather misinterpreted. A sign can only become a sign if it is interpreted as such, and although anything potentially can become a sign, nothing is *essentially* a sign in the sense of a natural kind (although a sign qua object may have essential characteristics—which is the gist of 2.247). Short seems to agree: "Nothing is

a sign in itself" (1981: 202). As I have been emphasizing here, something becomes a sign as soon as it meets these formal conditions. For the notion of degeneracy in Peirce, see Kruse (1991).

4. See also Peirce's earliest definitions which have the same idea (WP 2: 223, 3: 66–67).

5. Savan (1994: 186) seems to agree with this account: "the ground is that special *aspect* or *feature* of a thing which is selected by the interpretant as the clue suggesting its object. Perhaps we should not say that the ground is *selected* by the interpretant. It would be more accurate to say the ground is a *proposal*, a *hypothesis*, a means by which the interpretant can reach out toward its object." Prower (1986: 27 ff., 120) interprets Peirce's notion of ground as a "superordinate, abstractive, selective semiotic principle which regulates the valuation and selection of linguistic elements by making pertinent . . . only those predicates of a sign's object which are relevant to the signifier of the sign" (1986: 129). In this case the ground acts like a grid for what I have called transvaluation of the object by the sign (Liszka 1989).

6. The term "ground" is not continuously employed by Peirce. It is used in his early work on the categories and up to 1897, but it seems to drop out of sight after that. I do believe, however, that he uses the term "form" in place of it in his later writings, since it seems to play the same role: "I use the word 'Sign' in the widest sense for any medium for the communication or extension of a Form (or feature)" (LW 196). An early definition of ground suggests this connection: "By a *ground*, you remember, I meant the pure form or abstraction which is the original of the thing and of which the concrete thing is only the incarnation" (W 1: 474). An even earlier definition seems to suggest the same thing: "form is that respect in which a representation stands for a thing prescinded from all that can serve as the basis of a representation and therefore from its connection with the thing" (MS 802: 3).

7. Short (1982: 285) characterizes the ground in the following way: "something is a sign in virtue of a *ground*—or relation of sign to object—that would justify a particular interpretation of it." This seems to suggest that the ground *is* the establishment of the relation between sign and object, when in fact, that is more related to the job of the interpretant. My argument here is that the ground is the *presentation* of the object, rather than the establishment of the sign's connection with its object. As Greenlee writes, "What Peirce appears to have in mind is an idea as a *ground* of what I shall call 'abstraction.' In the representative relation abstraction obtains because representation is aspectual, requiring a point of view in terms of which an object is relevant to the significance of the sign" (1973: 64). However, as *presentation* of the object, the ground can then serve as the *basis* of the connection between sign and object established by the interpretant (cf. Savan 1994: 186, preceding note). It's not the ground that establishes the connection but the interpretant by means of, or on the basis of, that ground. To put it differently, presentation makes representation possible. If that is what Short means here, then there's no dispute. I think Savan's account of the ground agrees with this interpretation to some extent (1988: 19). He writes, "a sign, considered in itself, is the ground on which the object for which

it stands is interpreted by the sign into which it is translated, or transformed."
In other words this suggests that the ground is the basis of the interpretation
of the sign. Savan then goes on to say that "the ground of the sign is that
specific characteristic which is essential to its functioning as a sign" (1988: 19).
Probably a more accurate claim would have been to say that the ground of
the sign is the specific characteristic of the object presented in the sign, and so
serves as the basis for its function as representing the object: "the ground is a
proposal . . . a means by which the interpretant can reach out towards its
object" (1994: 186–7). Savan suggests that the ground of the sign is bound up
with its quality, that is, the first trichotomy in Peirce's typology of signs (cf.
1988: 19).

   8. Sometimes Peirce characterizes the dynamic object as the "real" object:
it is "the object as it is regardless of any particular aspect of it, the Object in
such a relation as unlimited and final study would show it to be" (CP 8.183;
cf. MS 318: 33). On the other hand, as late as 1909, in a letter to William
James, Peirce makes clear that he does not intend to characterize the dynamic
object solely as a "real"object: "We must distinguish between the Immediate
object, —i.e., the Object as represented in the sign,— and the Real (no, because
perhaps the Object is altogether fictive, I must choose a different term, therefore),
I say rather the dynamical Object . . . " (CP 8.314; cf. CP 5.473). Peirce also
hints at a third sort of object other than the immediate and the dynamic, which
he calls the *absolute* object: "the object at the limit of an endless series of
representations" (CP 1.359). It would be interesting to explore the relation
between this and the dynamic object.

   9. Sorting through this matter requires several complex distinctions among
reality, fiction, externality, actuality, and truth. First, the real is distinct from
the fictive. "If how we think of something can change the way it is," then it
is *fictive* (CP 6.328; cf. MS 333: 19, 372: 11, 609: 7, 683: 33). When Shakespeare
created the character of Hamlet, had he thought of Hamlet differently, then
Hamlet would have been different. The *real*, conversely, is, as Peirce is fond
of saying, that which it is regardless of what you or I or any finite number of
people think it is (CP 5.432). In other words, the real will be what it is
independently of our thoughts or opinions (CP 5.408). Something has *externality*
if it exists independently of any thought or sign process; or, to put it differently,
something is external if it does not have its origin in some sign process (CP
6.328). In other words, the external is not mental (CP 6.328), and so, by
implication, something mental or found within the sign process, is *internal.*
However, although the external and the real seem identical by definition, they
are not (CP 6.328, 7.339). It is quite possible that something mental is real
(MS 200: 4). For example, the fact of dreaming is real, although the content
is fictive (CP 5.405; cf. MS 852: 11). Peirce makes this clearer in the following
example: "Thus an emotion of the mind is real, in the sense that it exists in
the mind whether we are distinctly conscious of it or not. But it is not external
because although it does not depend upon what we think about it, it does
depend upon the state of our thoughts about something" (CP 7.339). Consequently, we can have something that is both externally and internally real:

Of realities, some are internal, some are external. An external reality is an object whose characters are not only independent of the thoughts of me or you about this object but are also independent of our thoughts about any other object; while an internal reality though not dependent on our opinions about it does depend upon some thought (MS 333: 19).

This distinction between external and internal reality is crucial for allowing that although mathematical objects are products of the mind, they are not fictional (cf. Dozoretz 1979: 81 ff.). Mathematics becomes, then, the paradigm of the internally real. Since mathematics involves showing a necessary connection from a beginning point to its consequence, then this serves to distinguish fictions—which are internal but not real—from the internally real (Dozoretz 1979: 82). Thus the relations among Hamlet's actions, so to speak, have no necessity, in the way in which there is a necessity between two plus two and four.

This interpretation allows a distinction, then, between the dynamic object and the real. The distinction between the external and internal allows Hamlet to serve just as much as a dynamic object as a rock. But the distinction between the internal and the internally real allows us to say that Hamlet is fictional, while granting mathematical systems a certain (general) reality.

The real is not independent of thought or semeiosis *in general*, according to Peirce, but only of *finite* thought; whereas the external is independent of any semeiosis (CP 5.408). The real, in many of Peirce's definitions "is that which, sooner or later, information and reasoning would finally result in . . . " (CP 5.311). It seems, then, that the real is realized, so to speak, in semeiosis of the highest sorts. As Peirce argues, "the highest grade of reality is only reached by signs" (LW 23). Thus the real is internal to the process of inquiry, but not dependent on any particular inquiry, but is something which final inquiry *would* realize. The real is the *would be* of the object of inquiry. In this regard, the dynamic object is the initial determinant of the sign (CP 1.339), while any information about the real is embedded within that process of sign-determination as found in the final point of inquiry.

The actual existent, on the other hand, is what is determinate (versus the possible) (CP 6.349). Hamlet is a nonactual object of which something, none-theless, can be said to be true, but George Washington was an actual existent, of whom also many things can be said to be true. "Existence, then, is a special mode of reality, which, whatever other characteristics it possesses, has that of being absolutely determinate. Reality, in its turn, is a special mode of being, the characteristic of which is that things that are real are whatever they really are, independently of any assertion about them" (CP 6.349).

On the problematics of Peirce's theory of the object, see Rosenthal (1990), Braga (1988), and Almeder (1968).

10. Unlike Goodman (1968: 5), for instance, who gives a narrower meaning to representation, understood as a species of denotation. The variety of senses of "representation" in Peirce is expressed in the following passage: "a word represents a thing to the concept in the mind of the hearer, a portrait represents

the person . . . to the conception of recognition, a weathervane represents the direction of the wind to the conception of he who understands it, a barrister represents his client to the judge and jury whom he influences" (CP 1.553).

11. This seems to be indicated in the following passage: "I define a Sign as anything which is so determined by something else, called its Object, and so determines an effect upon a person, which effect I call its Interpretant, that the latter is thereby mediately determined by the former. My insertion of 'upon a person' is a sop to Cerberus, because I despair of making my own broader conception understood" (LW 84).

12. The classical view in Peirce scholarship suggested that the divisions of the interpretant into immediate, dynamic, and final are paradigmatic, all other divisions being relatively synonymous or analogous with these categories. This is the view I'm supposing and defending here.

Fitzgerald (1966) was the first, as far as I know, to argue against this claim. He states instead that the emotional, energetic, and logical interpretants ought to be seen as a subdivision of dynamic interpretants, since they are *actual* effects upon interpreters (1966: 78). Short expands this argument by saying that *each* of the divisions of interpretants, immediate, dynamic, and final, may be subdivided into emotional, energetic, and final (1981: 213 ff.).

Fitzgerald gives the following support for his position. He claims that since the dynamic interpretant is defined by Peirce as "the *actual* [italics added] effect which the Sign, as a Sign, really determines" (CP 4.536) or, elsewhere, as "the *direct* [italics added] effect actually produced by a Sign upon an interpreter of it" (CP 4.536), then the emotional, energetic, and logical interpretants must be considered as species of the dynamic interpretant, since they are all defined as effects upon an interpreter. Thus the emotional interpretant is defined as "the first proper significate effect of a sign. . . . [It] may amount to not much more than the feeling of recognition; and in some cases, it is the only proper significate effect that the sign produces . . . " (CP 5.475). The energetic interpretant is "any further proper significate effect" which "involves an effort," either mental or muscular (CP 5.476).

Certainly it is true that Peirce gives definitions of the interpretant in terms of "effect," although this does not exhaust its characterization, as I have pointed out. But I think that a distinction should be made between the interpretant as effect and the possible *kind* of effect it has. The immediate, dynamic, and final interpretants are all defined in terms of *different* kinds of effects. The immediate interpretant is the "*unanalyzed* [italics added] effect" of a sign (LW: 110); the dynamic interpretant is the *direct* or *actual* effect of the sign (CP 4.536). On the other hand, the final interpretant's effect refers to the manner in which "the Sign tends to represent itself to be related to its Object" (CP 4.536). Or, to put it differently, its effect is to establish rules for interpreting agencies. In this case the dynamic interpretant is not the only interpretant which produces an effect, although it produces a *direct* or *actual* effect, as opposed to the kind of effects produced by the other interpretants. I believe there a confusion here in Fitzgerald's interpretation between a feeling, action, or thought as a singular interpretant, understood as *product*, and the emotional, energetic, or logical interpretant as *types* of interpretants. If a thought is the immediate, unanalyzed effect of a sign, that does not make it a logical interpretant, but rather it is an immediate interpretant which happens to be a thought. Since Peirce makes it very clear that "the [dynamical] interpretant derives its character from the Dyadic category, the category of Action" (CP 8.315), and since "action cannot be a logical interpretant" (CP 5.491), then the logical interpretant could not be a subdivision of the dynamic interpretant. "The dynamic interpretant is a *single*, actual event" (LW 111). A thought may be a single, actual event, but a single actual thought is never a logical interpretant.

This fundamental mistake by Fitzgerald is continued and expanded by Short. He argues that each immediate, dynamic, and final interpretant may be subdivided into emotional, energetic, and logical interpretants (1981: 213). He argues that since the immediate interpretant is the peculiar interpretability that a sign has, then it could be argued that

> the possibility in which the interpretability of a sign consists could be a possible feeling, a possible action, or a possible thought. . . . Similarly, those interpretants that are actually formed may be either feeling, acts, or words, thoughts or habits. It is true that a feeling in itself is something less than an actuality, while a law or habit is more than any set of actualities. Nevertheless, feelings do actually occur and habits and certain other laws do come to be formed, modified or destroyed. Therefore, a dynamic interpretant can be emotional or logical and need not in every case be energetic. Similarly, the final interpretant . . . could, depending on the sign and the goal of interpretation, be either the feeling or the act or the thought which *would be* the ideally adequate interpretant. Thus the two trichotomies intersect, yielding nine distinct types of interpretant. (1981: 213)

Again, as in the case of Fitzgerald, I would argue that it is a category mistake to classify a logical interpretant, which has the form of a rule or law or conceptual association, with the dynamic interpretant, which always has the form of a singular action or event. To say that a rule or habit *actually* forms, or is actualized, in an organism's behavior, i.e., is *present*, is not the same thing as saying that a single event or singular action *actually* occurs. For example, in the latter case, the wind may cause a windvane to point in a certain direction—that is an "actual singular event"—but this is much different than citing the conventional and physical laws and rules which allow interpreters to argue that the wind is moving in a northerly direction—such rules "actually" exist, but not as a singular, dyadic event. There is an equivocation in the word "actual" which is exploited by Short. In the first sense "actual" is opposed to "possible"; in the second sense, "actual" is opposed to "nonpresent."

By the same token, to argue that a singular action, which may be the energetic interpretant of a command, can be a final interpretant is to violate the nature of the lawlike character of such interpretants. A singular action can never be a law—only when such actions are organized into a regularity of such actions can a rule or law be ascribed to them. The same can be said of placing feeling in this category. I may be presented with a picture that simply disgusts me—and this may be the only effect that the sign has on me (i.e., there is no thought or action which accompanies the viewing of the picture), but what would make this feeling the final interpretant of the picture would be the context of its regular association with the picture.

Short's position is given some textual support in a passage from Peirce quoted by Johansen (1985: 247):

> The *Immediate interpretant* is the immediate pertinent possible effect in its unanalyzed primitive entirety. . . . It may be a quality of feeling, more or less vague or an idea of an effort . . . or it may be the idea of a form or anything of a general type. The *Dynamical interpretant* is the actual effect produced upon a given interpreter on a given occasion in a given stage of his consideration of the sign. This again may be 1st a feeling merely, or 2nd an action, or 3rd a habit. . . . (MS 339d: 546–547)

A careful reading of this passage shows that although Peirce suggests that feelings, acts, and thoughts (general ideas and habits) may be immediate or dynamical interpretants, he does not say thereby that emotional, energetic, and logical *interpretants* are subspecies of either immediate or dynamical interpretants. The mention of feelings, acts, and thoughts under the rubric of immediate and dynamic interpretants pays attention to their peculiar status: under the concept of immediate interpretant, it is the *quality* of feeling, a *vague idea* of action, and an *idea* of a general type, rather than the general type itself. It is then unlikely that an energetic interpretant, which is a definite, singular act, is of the same type as a "vague idea" of action. Under the concept of dynamical interpretant, Peirce considers feelings, acts, etc. as *actual* effects. The only anomalous piece in this puzzle is the mention of habit under dynamical inter-pretant. However, since its classification under dynamical interpretant makes it clear that habit is being considered as an *actual* effect, rather than habit per se, and since Peirce gives an example of how a single act may produce a habit (CP 5.477), this may not be that puzzling.

In addition to these considerations, Peirce's classification of interpretants—made in the context of the analysis of communication (LW 196)—strongly undermines the Fitzgerald/Short reading. How does this classification of inter-pretants fit into the nine divisions suggested by Short?

Although I have not examined every manuscript in this regard, it appears that Peirce's classification of interpretants occupies him after 1900 and shows a continuing experimentation with terminology as well as different kinds of classification:

1902 (CP 2.294): immediate
1904 (LW 34): immediate, dynamic
1905 (MS 339c: 504): dynamic
1906 (MS 339d: 546–547): immediate, dynamic, final
1906 (CP 5.475–476): emotional, energetic, logical, first logical, ultimate logical
1906 (MS 499: 47–48): immediate, naive or rogate, dynamical, normal

1906 (LW 196): intentional, effectual, communicational
1907 (MS 318: 35–37): emotional, energetic, logical
1908 (CP 8.344): immediate, dynamic, normal
1908 (CP 8.369–372): immediate or felt, dynamic, eventual
1908 (LW 84): destinate, effective, explicit
1909 (CP 8.314): immediate, dynamic, final or ultimate
1909 (LW 109–111): immediate, dynamic, final

The alternative to the Fitzgerald/Short interpretation is to suggest that Peirce was experimenting with various terminologies for three basic types of interpretants, that these terminologies complement one another, or both. It seems that both sorts of things are happening. On the one hand, there is simply different or slightly different terminology for the same basic distinction represented by the immediate-dynamic-final interpretant division. On the other hand, there seem to be divisions that concern specific types of semeioses, for example, emotional, energetic, and logical for human semeioses and intentional, effectual, and communication for semeiosis that deals specifically with communication. This might be analogous to the way in which he classifies the categories. There is the logical division of monad, dyad, triad; the metaphysical distinction of quality, fact, law; the phenomenological division of firstness, secondness, thirdness. Each set complements and clarifies the other.

Since Peirce makes the division between immediate, dynamic, and final and emotional, energetic, and logical around the same time, this would have been an ideal time for him to combine those divisions in the way that Short suggests—if that were his intention. But there doesn't seem to be any genuine textual support for Short's claim.

13. See Gentry (1952).

14. This is a term not used later on in his thought—I believe it gets incorporated into the idea of *signification*, which he adopts from Lady Welby (cf. LW 111).

15. Strictly speaking, Peirce applies this terminology to his analysis of the traditional logical study of *terms*. I'm giving it wider application here in saying that it applies to any sign treated as if it were a term. This language bias is also shared by Peirce (cf. CP 6.338).

16. In order to remain consistent with the four formal conditions of a sign, there are certain axioms that would follow from the mediation of sense and reference by information, and the general characterizations of depth, breadth, and information:

1. A sign can only provide an increase in information if (a) it shows the sense attributed to a certain object, set, or kind of objects extends to other objects or (b) it adds to the depth of the objects referred to. This follows from the rule cited by Peirce (CP 2.419), "that every increase of information is accompanied by an increase in depth or breadth, independently of the other quantity."
2. No sign can have either zero breadth or zero depth; that is, every sign will provide some information. This follows from the formal conditions of the sign—every sign must have an object and a

ground—and also Peirce's axiom (CP 2.419) "that, when there is no information, there is either no depth or no breadth and conversely"—that suggests that since every sign formally must have depth and breadth, that there is no sign which does not convey some information (in proportion to the "area" it creates between depth and breadth).

The classical problems that arise from this are to show that so-called purely referential signs, e.g., demonstrative pronouns or proper names, must be treated as having sense, while purely qualitative signs (such as musical sounds or blotches of color) must have reference. Peirce is not always consistent on these matters. Sometimes he does indicate that indices have nothing to do with meaning (cf. CP 4.56). Peirce does argue in some detail that proper names do have a sense. A proper name, for one who is not acquainted with the person to whom it refers, means simply an individual whom it has been agreed to designate by that name; but for someone acquainted with the person referred to, the meaning of the proper name is quite extensive (CP 2.432).

17. As Skagestad writes, "Peirce was fully cognizant of the objection which was to be eloquently put by Russell in his criticism of Frege, namely, that within one and the same language the reference of a term can be picked out only through the meaning of that term, and the meaning of the term can be specified only through a description of its referent" (1981: 129).

18. Savan (1994: 184) argues similarly: "A sign is *triadic*. Three terms, ground, object and interpretant, are related to one another by three kinds of relations, monadic, dyadic and triadic. Each of these, terms and relations, is indispensable and irreducible." See also Kolaga: "the interdependence of the categories within the sign is thus of the structural type; an elimination of one destroys the triad. A sign is a sign only in virtue of its relations to the other two elements, and is qualified by these elements" (1986: 23).

19. See Fitzgerald (1966: 73 ff.); and cf. Seager (1988).

20. As Short puts it, "the likelihood of B's leading to an event of some type C has an influence on whether A produces B" (1981: 205). Von Wright makes a similar distinction between caused and intentional behavior (1971: 87 f.): an action may be distinguished in its outer and its inner aspects. Consider the action of opening a window by some agent. For convenience, let's suppose that the outer aspect has three phases, the pressing of a button (A), the opening of the window (B), and a drop in the temperature in a certain room (C). Thus the agent pressed the button and as a consequence the room was cooled, that is, A caused B and B caused C. But, as von Wright emphasizes, though this could obviously account for the causal relations between events, it does not explain why the agent opened the window (cf. Peirce's similar remarks in MS 1343: 26–27). He opened the window in order to cool the room, and the intention of the agent connects the phases of the outer action into a synthetic whole which cannot be reduced to an addition of relations between them. Even if one were to treat it as a cause, the explanation of why the agent performed the action would not result. We would simply have another preceding cause added to the series of dyadic relations: I (intention) causes A causes B causes

C. I caused A, A caused B, B caused C, but C, then, could not be understood as a reason for the action but only as the consequence of B. Intentional description involves the triadic relation between intention, result, and action and cannot be reduced to a series of causal relations between the outer phases of the action.

21. I'm referring to the following passage: "Every sufficiently complete symbol is a final cause and 'influences' real events, in precisely the same sense in which my desire to have the window open, that is, the symbol in my mind of the agreeability of it, influences the physical facts of my rising from my chair, going to the window and opening it" (NEM 4: 254).

22. Fitzgerald (1966: 73) makes the divisions somewhat differently than I've done here: (1) when the interpretant is triadically produced but is not predominantly thirdness, we have a "sign in the broad sense," and (2) where the interpretant is either a First, Second, or Third, but is not triadically produced, it is only a "quasi-sign." In support of the distinctions I'm making here, see Short (1982: 298–299): "There are signs throughout nature, but there are legisigns only where there is life, and legisigns always exist in order to serve the purposes of living things. Conventional legisigns, created and manipulated by individuals in ways that constantly produce new meanings, are distinctive—perhaps constitutive—of the form of consciousness found in human life."

23. See n. 3, this chapter.

24. Compare Michael Shapiro's remarks on this matter: "the triadic conception of sign which marks Peirce's theory is, therefore, inseparable from goal-directedness. Indeed, when Peirce speaks of the action of a sign as being triadic (CP 5.472–74), he means to equate triadic action with final causation, and to contrast it with dyadic action equated with efficient causation. . . . A sign may or may not be triadically produced. The difference between signs that are and signs that are not triadically produced in effect comes down to the presence or nonpresence, respectively, of a goal relative to which sign-action occurs. . . . The triadic character of a sign is thus inalienable from an encompassing goal-directed process in which interpretants of the sign may be formed and by which it may be interpreted as signifying an object. . . . From this it follows that sign-interpretation—semeiosis—is teleological" (Shapiro 1991: 23). This suggests that if the interpretant is not triadically produced but dyadically so, then the semeioses is not truly intentionally purposeful. Thus there may be semeioses whose interpretants are not intentionally directed but mechanically (dyadically) produced. In that case, the last claim that "semeiosis is teleological" would have to be modified to suggest that not all semeiosis is teleological, understood in the sense of the term used here.

25. Compare Johansen (1993: 133) on this matter: "There is a vast difference between the nuptial colors of the Stickleback and human speech . . . due to the difference on the one hand between an innate, limited, and inflexible instinctual semiotic competence, and on the other a learning capacity that makes habit-changes possible." This points out the difference between an indurated and a conventional habit of interpretation; however, evolutionary theory would suggest that the indurated habit is not entirely inflexible.

26. See Sebeok (1979).

27. Peirce scholars have been interested in accounting for the changes in these typologies. Savan (1977) suggests that they are due primarily to a significant change in Peirce's semeiotic theory. More specifically, (1) Peirce's concept of sign changes from its characterization as simply an element in the process of inference to the broader concept of it as a relative in a triadic process (1977: 187). (2) The relation of signs to the categories changes, such that in the early account, the categories are modeled precisely on the character of signs, so that being and representation are, for all purposes, synonymous (1977: 183); in the later account, the relation of signs to the categories changes (probably due to the development of Peirce's phenomenology and his expanded study of the logic of relations, and the position of phenomenology to logic as a discipline) so that signs are seen as a species of the broader category of relations. Moreover, the categories themselves are understood as ordinal positions in a triadic relation; consequently signs (objects and interpretants) are, too (1977: 189). (3) There is also a significant change in the interpretant, from the view of it as simply a leading principle in a process of inference to the idea of it as a self-corrective, evolutionary process toward the establishment of habits, regularities, and laws (1977: 190). (4) There is a change in the concept of the object, from its more formal role as correlate to a sign to its more dynamic role as the fundamental determinant of the semeiotic process (1977: 192).

Synthesizing these factors and extrapolating a bit, Savan's argument for the change in the typologies seems to be the suggestion that a broader understanding of signs as triadic relations and the understanding of semeiotic processes as dynamic, self-corrective processes induces Peirce to modify and expand his original typology of signs. Because of the broader understanding of triadic relations, a sign must also be understood in terms of its firstness (its inherent qualities, hence the first trichotomy in the interim typology), its secondness, and its thirdness (and so the change from one trichotomy to at least three). Because of the change in the understanding of the interpretant from simply a rule of inference to the more elaborate view of it as a self-corrective and developing process, argument and inference really belong to the third trichotomy, the relation of sign to interpretant and the relation of the sign to its various interpretants (hence the additional three trichotomies in the final version). Because the object plays a more dynamic role in the semeiotic process (undoubtedly due to the change from "nominalism" to realism), it is important to stress the relation of the sign to its dynamic object (as opposed to its immediate object) and so the justification in the final version of the two additional trichotomies.

In general, then, the changes from the original to the final typologies are motivated by: (1) a refinement of the categories through phenomenology, so that signs must be understood in terms of not only their thirdness but also their firstness and secondness; (2) a desire to see logic as a more comprehensive discipline than just the study of arguments, since the interpretant is not simply inference but is understood in the more comprehensive category of self-corrective process; (3) the change from nominalism to realism, which allows a more important role to the object as the determinant of semeiotic processes. This might be summarized in Peirce's own words:

> In a paper of 1867 May 14 ["On a New List of Categories"], I defined logic as the doctrine of the formal conditions of the truth of symbols; i.e., of the reference of symbols to their objects. Later, when I had recognized that science consists in *inquiry*, not in "doctrine", . . . I saw that for a long time those who devoted themselves to discovering the truth about the general reference of symbols to their objects would be obliged to make researches into the reference to their interpretants, too, as well as into other characters of symbols, and not *of symbols alone* but of all sorts of signs. So that, for the present, the man who makes researches into the reference of symbols to their objects will be forced to make original studies into all branches of the general theory of signs. . . . (LW: 79–80; repeated somewhat differently in LW: 118).

The development and changes in Peirce's thought have been subject to much study. Although Savan's account is specific to changes relevant in Peirce's semeiotic theory, for more general accounts one should refer to Max Fisch (1986: 227 ff.) and Murphey (1961: 3 ff.).

28. Not much is mentioned about sign typology after this early work. For example, in 1870 the only types of signs mentioned are the original ones, icons, indices, and symbols (W 2: 446), which Peirce calls the most fundamental and also the one most frequently used (CP 8.368, 2.275). Three years later, in an unpublished manuscript he seems to be on the verge of creating a prototype of the three divisions made later in the 1903 interim typology. Here he stresses the three conditions essential to a sign: (1) its material quality, (2) its *real* (as opposed to just its physical or actual) connection with its objects, either through genuine likeness, physical causation, or law; and that (3) a sign must be interpreted as such by some mind or interpreter (W 3: 67).

29. Peirce mentions in a draft of a letter to Lady Welby, dated December 24, 1908 (cf. CP 8.363), that "from 1905–1906 I devoted much study to my ten trichotomies of signs." The fullest expression of this final typology appears in this draft, which did not reach Lady Welby for some reason, and a letter dated a day earlier, which did reach her. In the final version there are now ten typologies or divisions.

1. According to the mode of apprehension of the sign (CP 8.344); this is the presentative aspect of the sign presented in the interim typology; instead of qualisign, sinsign, legisign, we now have *potisign, actisign,* and *famisign*; the characterization of the potisign is somewhat different than the analysis of the qualisign, since the emphasis is on possibility rather than the quality of sign.
2. According to the mode of presentation of the immediate object (CP 8.344). This includes *descriptives*, signs which state the characters of their objects, *designatives*, which direct attention to the object, and *copulants*, which express the logical relations of the object referred to in the sign.

3. According to the mode of being of the dynamical object (CP 8.344); if the sign refers to a possible, then it is an *abstractive*; if it refers to an occurrence, then it is a *concretive*; and if it refers to collections, then it is called a *collective*.
4. According to the relation of the sign to its dynamic object (CP 8.344); this is identical to the second trichotomy of *icon, index* and *symbol* in the interim typology.

Except for those previously articulated in the interim typology, the next six types are either sketched or simply left undefined.

5. According to the mode of presentation of the immediate interpretant (CP 8.344); if it gives utterance to feeling, then it is called *ejaculative*; *imperative* and *significative* are both left undefined (cf. Savan 1988: 53–54 for an attempt at their characterization).
6. According to the mode of being of the dynamic interpretant; the three are named, *sympathetic, shocking* and *usual*, but they are left undefined (cf. Savan 1988: 55–59 for an attempt at their characterization).
7. According to the relation of the sign to its dynamic interpretant (CP 8.344), or as Peirce says elsewhere, "the manner of appeal" (CP 8.370); *suggestive, imperative*, and *indicative* are the names used, but they are left undefined (cf. Savan 1988: 59–60 for an attempt at their characterization).
8. According to the mode of being of the normal or final interpretant (CP 8.344), or as Peirce says elsewhere, "the purpose of the eventual interpretant" (CP 8.372). *Gratific* is the name for the first division, but it is left undefined; the other two are not named but briefly described: "to produce action," "to produce self-control" (cf. Savan 1988: 64–65 and Shapiro 1983: 57 for attempts at their characterization).
9. According to the relation of the sign to the normal interpretant (CP 8.344); or, as to "the nature of the influence of the sign" (CP 8.373). This is a type identical to the division among rheme, dicisign, and argument in the interim typology; but now they are called, respectively, *seme, pheme*, and *delome*.
10. According to the triadic relation of the sign to its dynamic object and normal interpretant (CP 8.344); elsewhere he describes it "as to the nature of the assurance of an utterance" (CP 8.374). They are briefly described as assurance of instinct, assurance of experience, and assurance of form (cf. Savan 1988: 67–72 and Shapiro 1983: 60 for attempts at their characterization).

There are a number of scholarly puzzles and anomalies about this final typology that are undoubtedly generated because of its sketchy nature. For one thing, unlike the interim typology—which emphasizes the formal, relational aspects among sign, object, and interpretant, the final typology seems to include extra-formal considerations. The typology here involves "the mode of apprehension" of the sign, the "mode of presentation" of the immediate object, "the nature of the influence," "the purpose," the "manner of appeal." In other words the final typology is not concerned with the purely relational characteristics of all the correlates of sign relations but with these correlates as appreciated by the "mind of its interpreter" (CP 8.345). Why this appeal to mental language in this typology? Muller's (1994: 145) explanation of this matter is unsatisfactory. He suggests that the expansion in the final typology and its reformulation in psychological terms are due to the fact that, after 1903, "Peirce became more involved in questions dealing with the way we think" (1994: 145). But, of course, that was always Peirce's concern. The issue here is not how we think, but why Peirce would forego the more formalistic analysis of signs in the interim typology in favor of a more mentalistic one. There is not textual support for Muller's claim.

Besides the puzzle with the mentalistic language, it is also not clear why Peirce emphasizes the phenomenological or ontological status of the correlates in the sign process in the final typology. It is concerned with the "mode of being" of the dynamical object, the "mode of being" of the dynamical interpretant, and the "nature" of the normal or final interpretant.

Another puzzle concerning the final typology is how it is that Peirce moves from three divisions in the interim typology to six in the expanded to ten in the final. What principle or idea is underlying the changes in the sign divisions? We've already examined the theoretical reasons for the change (in n. 27), but what are the specific reasons for the number of trichotomies? One of the theoretical justifications suggested by Savan and mentioned earlier is the desire to analyze the sign in its fuller phenomenological sense, not only in its thirdness but in its secondness and firstness as well. Using that as a clue, it would seem that the fullest treatment of the sign would be to analyze the sign-object-interpretant in all its possible relations. Peirce's rule is that every triadic relationship involves, in addition to the triadic relationship itself, three dyadic ones and three monadic characters (CP 6.331). Thus the sign-object-interpretant relation should have seven aspects all together if it were analyzed with this rule in mind: the sign, object, and interpretant considered in themselves, the sign-object, sign-interpretant, and object-interpretant relations, and the sign-object-interpretant relation itself. In the interim typology, Peirce only selects three of these possibilities. Strictly speaking, one could also include the object in itself, the interpretant in itself, the relation between object and interpretant, and the sign-object-interpretant relation. It seems, then, that Peirce is not interested in analyzing the sign-object-interpretant relation in all its aspects in the context of *sign* typology, but only those which directly involve the sign as a member of the relation, although even this explanation would not account for why the sign-object-interpretant relation is left out of the interim typology. Thus the analysis of the inherent characteristics of the object and of the interpretant, and of the relation between object and interpretant, is carried out by Peirce outside the context of *sign* typology.

This same principle—only those aspects of the triadic relation which directly include the sign as a member are to be considered—seems also to be consistently applied in the expanded typology. However, given the refinements made in the analysis of the object and the interpretant, additional typologies are needed. Once the object is subdivided into dynamic and immediate and the interpretant into its three subtypes, the relations that involve the sign are increased to six: sign, sign–dynamic object, sign–immediate object, sign–immediate interpretant, sign–dynamic interpretant, sign–final interpretant.

In the final typology, this is refined even further. Not only is there the relation of the sign to the dynamic object, but now there is the relation of the sign to the dynamic object *as* a phenomenological type: if the dynamic object is a possible, then the sign of it is an abstractive; if the dynamic object is an existent, then the sign of it is a concretive; and if it is a collection, then the sign of it is a collective. Further refinements are made in regard to the dynamic and final interpretant. Now not only is there the relation of the sign to the dynamic interpretant, but there is also a relation of the sign to the dynamic interpretant *as* having a certain mode of being; similarly for the final interpretant.

But there is something still puzzling about the last typology, in the sense that, given the guide for the other typologies, there may not simply be enough trichotomies. That is, if Peirce were to consistently follow the rule which seems to guide the previous typologies ("of all the possible relations in the semiotic process, include only those that have the sign as a member of the relation"), then several additional trichotomies should be included. Let me try to retrace the thinking here.

Given the number of correlatives and the triadic relations involved, as illustrated in figure 2 (see text), there are three triads involved (and using the abbreviations indicated in figure 1):

S-IO-II
S-DO-DI
S-DO-FI

Given Peirce's rule, that every triadic relationship involves one triadic relation, three dyadic ones, and three monadic characters (CP 6.331), every triad would have seven relationships to consider. Given that there are three such triadic relationships in this model, that would make twenty-one altogether. However, if we subtract the redundancies (two cases of the monadic character of the sign, two cases of the monadic character of the dynamic object, and one case of the sign–dynamic object relation), then that leaves sixteen. However, we could conceivably include the dyadic relations between correlatives in the respective triads not already accounted for, for example, DO-IO. We should also consider the dyadic relations among the three triads, for example, [S-IO-II]-[S-DO-DI]. Finally, there would also be the triadic relation among the three triads. I calculate this as a grand total of twenty-eight typologies, which I list in figure 3.

Excluding those that do not have the sign as a member of its relation leaves thirteen, three more than in the final typology. However, if we keep in mind that Peirce also creates typologies which concern the relation of the sign not only to each of the other correlates but also to each of the other correlates *as* a phenomenological type, there are at least three additional trichotomies not listed here. Consequently, there are really six trichotomies that are excluded from the final typology that should be included on the basis of rules consistent with the previous typologies. It seems, then, that the exclusion of trichotomies

S	IO	II
S-IO	IO-DO	II-DI
S-DO	IO-II	II-FI
S-II	IO-DI	DI
S-DI	IO-FI	DI-FI
S-FI	DO	FI
S-IO-II	DO-II	
S-DO-DI	DO-DI	
S-DO-FI	DO-FI	
[S-IO-II]-[S-DO-DI]		
[S-IO-II]-[S-DO-FI]		
[S-DO-DI]-[S-DO-FI]		
[S-IO-II]-[S-DO-DI]-[S-DO-FI]		

Key: S=sign, IO=immediate object, DO=dynamic object, II=immediate interpretant, DI=dynamic interpretant, FI=final interpretant

Figure 3. Possible relations among the components of the sign.

from consideration is based on a rather puzzling and mysterious criterion, at least one that is not consistent with the guides for the other typologies.

For all these reasons, and despite Savan's interesting guesses at the characterization of signs involved in these typologies, I think that we have to agree with Short (1982: 306) that although there is promise here, there are many problems, contradictions, and confusions in the very general and sketchy character of the final typology.

30. This becomes better known in British analytic philosophy as the "type-token" distinction, thanks primarily to the influence of F. P. Ramsey. On this matter, see Hardwick (1979: 27).

31. Peirce also called an icon a "likeness" (CP 1.558). Ransdell (1979: 55) notes a subtle distinction in Peirce among *icon, iconic sign,* and *hypoicon.* An icon is, phenomenologically speaking, always a first. A map of a terrain, since it is an existent, could not, strictly speaking, be counted as an icon. However, it can act as an iconic sign, which Peirce wants to call a *hypoicon* (cf. CP 2.276). Ransdell clarifies the distinction in the following way: "An *icon* is any possible qualitative content of consciousness—what Peirce calls a 'Firstness'—considered in respect to its possible function in cognition as the form (that is, quality or character) *of* an actual or possible object. An *iconic sign* ('hypoicon') is anything whatever which does or can function as a sign in virtue of its embodiment of some icon proper." See also Short (1982: 291). For the sake of convenience I'll forgo this subtle distinction in favor of using the term icon for all instances of similarity in signs regardless of phenomenological status.

32. On the issue of metaphor in Peirce, see Haley (1988, 1993) and Anderson (1984).

33. For a detailed analysis of these various features and their shortcomings, see Goudge (1965).

34. The symbol is not always conventional but could be the result of a natural disposition, or indurated habit (cf. CP 2.297). See Short (1982: 296 ff.), who discusses this matter in regard to the legisign. See also the earlier discussion in this volume on the difference among semeioses in which the interpretant is triadically rather than dyadically produced.

35. There is some qualification to this claim (cf. CP 2.341). Here Peirce seems to suggest that every general sign, even a "term," involves at least a rudimentary assertion.

36. For further discussion of the character of propositions, see the following studies on Peirce's theory of propositions: Berry (1952), Hilpinen (1992), Feibleman (1969), Houser (1992), Short (1984).

37. See Lieb (1953: 47).

38. See Lieb (1953: 48).

39. This can be expressed by the formula $\sum_{n=1}^{t+1} n$, where t = the number of trichotomies. For 3 trichotomies of signs that would make 10 classes, for 10 trichotomies of signs, as in the final typology, that would make 66 classes of signs.

40. The term "qualification rule" is used by Savan (1988: 14).

41. As mentioned in n. 39, using 10 trichotomies of signs suggested by the final typology instead of 3 would produce 66 classes of signs (cf. Weiss and Burks 1945). This is complicated by the fact that each of the 66 classes would have 10 aspects (corresponding to one of each of the 10 trichotomies)—and there is the problem of how these aspects are to be ordered; see the disagreement among Weiss and Burks (1945), Sanders (1970: 11), and Muller (1994: 147).

42. This is expressed by Peirce in the fact that in his chart of signs (CP 2.264), certain aspects of the sign are made bold.

43. See figure 4.

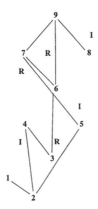

Figure 4. Diagram of the relations of inclusion. Numbers refer to the ten classes of signs listed in the text. R = reference, I = information.

44. So Peirce's example of a feeling of red (CP 2.254) is still an instantiation and so really an iconic sinsign rather than a qualisign as he suggests.

3. Critical Logic

1. This is certainly the view held by Skagestad (1981: 77 ff.).

2. According to Peirce, the "pragmaticist answers the question of correspondence in this way" (CP 5.553). The pragmatic maxim, if somewhat extrapolated, suggests that the meaning of a sign is the meaning of its effects or consequences (cf. CP 5.402, 5.404). As Skagestad (1981: 125 ff.) suggests, Peirce's early work on signs can be seen as a preliminary formulation of the pragmatic maxim; for example, Peirce talks about the meaning of a thought-sign as the infinite train of subsequent thoughts in which it may be interpreted (cf. CP 5.289). On this matter see also Altschuler (1978), Gallie (1952: 137), and Wennerberg (1962: 147).

3. Fisch (1978: 45) shows how this definition gets modified in Peirce to include also the development of the hypothesis and not just its necessary consequences. In 1896, Peirce offers the following qualification of this definition:

> Mathematics may be defined as the study of the substance of exact hypotheses. It comprehends 1st, the framing of hypotheses, and 2nd, the deduction of their consequences. . . . The definition I here propose differs from that of my father only in making mathematics to comprehend the framing of the hypotheses as well as the deduction from them. (MS 16: 1; cf. MS 18: 30 and NEM 2: 595; for an explanation of this, see CP 3.559)

Indeed, Fisch (1978: 41–49), gives a step-by-step development of Peirce's notion of mathematical reasoning and its relation to semeiotic. See also Murphey (1961) and Ketner and Putnam (1992).

4. Cf. Houser (1992: xvi) on this matter: "In his later years, Peirce . . . came to associate much of what we would today call mathematical logic with mathematics; logic, on the other hand, he came to regard as a normative science concerned with intellectual goodness. . . . "

5. I'm following Feibleman's analysis here (1969: 113). However, I'm not sure if there is a difference in Peirce between inference and leading principle; Feibleman shows no textual support for the difference.

6. Peirce sees this in its modern conditional form: If A, then B; but A; therefore B (cf. CP 5.276).

7. See Ketner (1985: 409).

8. Cf. Niiniluoto (1993).

9. See Ketner (1985); and cf. Zeman (1986). Sowa (forthcoming) has argued that the existential graphs are superior to other systems of logic for the representation of discourse and the study of language, although Peirce seemed to think they had a more limited use.

10. See Ketner (1985), Roberts (1964), and Sowa (forthcoming) on existential graphs.

11. There is an extensive literature on both the confirmation of hypotheses generally and on Peirce's analysis of the matter. For the former, some of the more notable accounts are given by Hempel (1965), Salmon (1984), and Van Fraasen (1980). On the topic of Peirce and induction, see the following: Braithwaite (1934), Goudge (1940), Burks (1964), Lenz (1964), Cheng (1966), and Merrill (1975).

12. Cf., for example, the difference between the assessments in CP 2.632 and in 2.102 and 2.755; also see Anderson (1986: 150 ff.). I'm not interested here in tracing the scholarly evolution of this change in view; instead I'll be mostly concerned with the mature view. Those who wish to trace this evolution can refer to Fann (1970). On the matter of Peirce and abduction, see also Burks (1946), Alexander (1965), Sharpe (1970), Ayim (1974), Thagard (1977), Brown (1983), and Staat (1993).

13. Wegener (1966: 1).

14. See Hempel (1966, chap. 1).

15. See related work in DiPaolo et al. (1991).

16. See Liszka (1991).

17. See Haley (1988: 52, 53), Andersen (1980), and Shapiro and Shapiro (1976).

18. Savan, for example, notes that deductive inference "is essential to mediate the connection between the abduction of an hypothesis and its testing through induction" (1994: 193).

19. There are other senses also; see CP 2.422n1.

20. The case is from Klawans (1991).

21. Compare Hawking's remark (1993: 135): " . . . Darwin's idea of natural selection would lead us to the correct answer. Maybe the correct answer is not the right way to describe it, but natural selection should at least lead us to a set of physical laws that work fairly well."

22. See Skakgestad (1981: 171).

23. See Habermas (1972: 119); see also Misak (1994: 764 ff.) for a discussion of Peirce's antitranscendental justification of the leading principles of inquiry.

24. See Misak (1994: 764) on this point: "certain principles are justified because without them, we could not go on. Peirce is fond of this . . . sort of argument."

25. Kant (1956: 127).

4. Universal Rhetoric

1. Some general studies of Peirce's rhetoric include a master's thesis by Johnson (1968). See also a dissertation by Lyne (1978). Feibleman (1969) presents a concise summary. See also Savan (1988a).

2. Interestingly, this is the branch (as Peirce understands it) of semeiotics that is of the most current interest. Many who ally themselves in some way with the theory of semeiotics are primarily concerned with the whole issue of inquiry and knowledge, especially its growth, development, origin, and understanding within the communities in which it is engaged. The work of Michel Foucault would be the primary example of this sort of effort.

3. But compare CP 1.445, where the definition is given to critical logic. See Houser (1992a: xxxix).

4. See Booth (1988). Coduction could be thought of as a species of rhetorical argument which uses induction, deduction, and abduction but within the context of a cooperative effort *inter homines*, in which, in principle, collateral experience, intersubjective norms, advice, intuition, personal relations, feelings, emotions interact over time to produce and revise judgments.

5. Peirce, as far as I know, makes only one division of speculative rhetoric (MS 774: 13–15). This is (1) according to the special nature of the ideas to be surveyed. This in turn is subdivided in the following way:

(a) the rhetoric of fine art, that is, the matter of feeling
(b) the rhetoric of practical persuasion
(c) the rhetoric of science, where the matter is knowledge
   (i) rhetoric of communication of discoveries
      (a) with respect to mathematics
      (b) with respect to philosophy
      (c) with respect to science
   (ii) the rhetoric of scientific digests
      (a) with respect to the rhetoric of speech and language
   (iii) the rhetoric of applications to special kinds of purposes
      (a) rhetoric of signs to be translated into human thought

The other divisions include (2) according to the special class of signs to be interpreted, the special medium of communication, and (3) according to the special nature of the class of signs into which the interpretations is to take place. In this apparently tentative division, there is no real elaboration by Peirce of what exactly these divisions mean. I am arguing here, however, that if univeral rhetoric concerns the relation of signs to interpretants, it makes sense that there would be at least three subdivisions, based on the three principal types of interpretants, something which is hinted at in the subdivision of (1) above.

6. Cf. Savan (1981). Based on fragments in Peirce, Savan argues for a distinction among "natural emotions," such as natural fears, revulsion, joy; "a second class of emotions," which are acquired through socialization, such as moral indignation; and sentiments, which are "enduring and ordered systems of emotions, attached either to a person, an institution, or, in Peirce's case, a method." These include the so-called logical sentiments (see Savan 1988: 330–331). Sentiments, especially logical sentiments, are ways of fixing emotions and stabilizing beliefs in our lives (1988: 331).

7. There is a possibility that Peirce's notion of the *commens* is related to Kant's notion of the *sensus communis* and its venerable tradition. In Kant (1974: 136), the *sensus communis*, is

> a sense common to all, i.e., a faculty of judgment which, in its reflection, takes account (a priori) of the mode of representation of all other men in thought, in order, as it were, to compare its judgment with the collective reason of humanity.... This is done by comparing

our judgment with the possible rather than the actual judgments of others, and by putting ourselves in the place of any other man, by abstracting from the limitations which contingently attach to our own judgment.

The sensus communis would be that which generates both a moral community and a community of inquiry. Kant likens the sensus communis to *taste*, which is what makes feeling universally communicable. For the older tradition, starting with Vico, see a concise account given by Gadamer (1975: 19 ff.). For Vico, as Gadamer explains, the sensus communis does not mean only that general faculty in all humans, but the sense that founds community. The notion of sensus communis is tied to the practice of rhetoric. Shaftesbury and Reid, according to Gadamer, adopt the notion to mean the sense of the general good and the love of the community, natural affection, humanity, and obligatoriness.

8. Dewey (1973: 636) articulates this idea very well by showing how the possibility of having signs makes possible a community:

> Only when there exist *signs* or *symbols* of activities and of their outcome can the flux [of experience] be viewed as from without, be arrested for consideration and esteem, and be regulated. . . . As symbols are related to one another, the important relations of a course of events are recorded and are preserved as meanings. Recollection and foresight are possible; the new medium facilitates calculation, planning, and a new kind of action which intervenes in what happens to direct its course in the interest of what is foreseen and desired. . . . Events cannot be passed from one to another, but meanings may be shared by means of signs. Wants and impulses are then attached to common meanings. They are thereby transformed into desires and purposes which, since they implicate a common or mutually understood meaning, present new ties, converting a conjoint activity into a community of interest and endeavor.

9. Royce apparently sent Peirce a copy of *The Problem of Christianity*; Peirce received it in May 1913 and read it in some detail, according to one of Royce's letters (see Clendenning and Oppenheim 1990: 140). The letter also states Peirce's approval of the general ideas there, especially in regard to Royce's use of Peirce's theory of signs (Clendenning and Oppenheim 1990: 140). As Apel (1981: 135) writes on this matter, "Royce's idea of the 'community of interpreters,' expounded in the second volume of his last work, *The Problem of Christianity* (1913), provides perhaps the most important single contribution to the extension and development in hermeneutic and social philosophical terms of Peirce's semiotic." See also Corrington (1984) on Royce's notion of community.

10. See Royce (1968: 253).

11. Royce wants to make communication a second formal condition for the possibility of community: "The second condition upon which the existence of a community depends is the fact that there are in the social world a number of distinct selves capable of social communication, and, in general, engaged in

communication" (1968: 255). Dewey seems to agree on this matter (1973: 625): "But participation in activities and sharing in results are additive concerns. They demand *communication* as a prerequisite."

12. See Dewey (1973: 624–625): "Whenever there is a conjoint activity whose consequences are appreciated as good by all singular persons who take part in it, and where the realization of the good is such as to effect an energetic desire and effort to sustain it in being just because it is a good shared by all, there is in so far a community." "'We' and 'our' exist only when the consequences of combined action are perceived and become an object of desire and effort . . . " (p. 625).

13. See Royce (1968: 256).

14. See Schiller (1965: 138): " . . . Beauty alone can confer on [humankind] a *social character*. Taste alone brings harmony into society, because it establishes harmony in the individual." Compare this idea with Kant's notion of the *sensus communis* (see n. 7, this chapter). Also compare this with the analysis of Schiller given very early by Peirce: "[Beauty] places the mind in a state of "infinite determinableness" so that it can turn in any direction and is in perfect freedom, hence, beauty is in the highest degree fruitful with respect to knowledge and morality" (W 1: 12). This is later developed as the "play of musement," which corresponds to Schiller's notion of *Spieltrieb*, the essence of which, according to Peirce, is the liberty of thought (cf. CP 6.460). To this end, Peirce certainly sees an important role for the rhetoric of fine art (cf. MS 774: 13). The rhetoric of fine art, to the extent that it deals with questions of feeling, aesthetic response, and the like, would be an appropriate subdivision of this aspect of universal rhetoric (cf. MS 774: 13).

15. Cf. Schiller (1965: 73 ff.).

16. See Lyne (1980).

17. Savan (1981: 7) expresses these logical sentiments in the following way:

> It is a matter of faith or trust that there is a real world which is independent of what any man or finite group of men may think it to be. It is a matter of hope that this independent reality can be known eventually through the long painstaking process [of inquiry]. . . . [And] the scientist must also be moved by the love of truth, that is to say, by a willing sacrifice of personal short-term achievement for the long-run approximation to an ideally ultimate and stable truth, agreed upon by the scientific community.

See also Savan (1965: 44–50).

18. See LW 197, where Peirce claims that existential graphs, which are the best formulation for Peirce of inferencing, cannot express the communication of propositions.

19. See Brock (1981: 319).

20. See also CP 4.6. See Johansen (1993: 190 ff.) on this matter. As Andacht (1994) suggests, in order for communication to take place, there must be a substitutability of speaker and utterer, a possibility of exchanging roles.

21. See chap. 2 on the question of quasi-signs and quasi-minds. It might be argued that a dyadic process, such as a cause-and-effect relation, is transformed

into a transmission when an interpreter, capable of triadic action, or being a quasi-mind, or capable of being affected by a quasi-sign in Peirce's sense, is present, that is, a sign-interpreting agency capable of having that object creates an interpretant within it (either dyadically or triadically); transmission is transformed into a communication when both utterer and interpreter are present, both of which are capable of triadic action (either as genuine or quasi-minds). Thus organic, cybernetic, or even servomechanisms are capable of transmission, that is, activity that is not purely dyadic, although not communication. Human beings, among other species capable of genuine, i.e., convention-capable minds, are capable of communication.

22. As Michael Shapiro (1991: 27–28) argues, that which is essential, at least to the existence of a legisign, is an interpreter that interprets legisigns as the utterer does and a replicator that replicates legisigns as the utterer does, so as to elicit those specific interpretations. "There is thus a nexus of mutual presuppositions: replicator and interpreter each presuppose each other; legisigns and the existence of a legisign presuppose both replicators and interpreters."

23. See Johansen (1993: 190 ff.) on this matter.

24. This is a definition of the immediate interpretant, which Peirce likens to Welby's notion of "sense" (LW 110).

25. See Brock (1981).

26. We might then speculate that Peirce's response to the puzzles presented by Russell's enigmatic proposition "the present king of France is bald" might be similar to Strawson's, not as to the truth or falsity of the proposition, but in the sense that most likely any present-day speaker would claim that there is no king of France. To the extent that such a description corresponds to nothing in the universe of discourse or the collateral experience of the interpreter, it is meaningless for that interpreter. In this respect, Peirce might agree with Kripke's assessment that "reference actually seems to be determined by the fact that the speaker is a member of a community of speakers who use the name" (1972: 106).

27. As Brock comments on this matter, "relative to such a universe of discourse and such conventions, proper names and definite descriptions are *determinate* in reference. But they are not *absolutely determinate*, i.e., they are not determinate in all conceivable universes of discourse" (1979: 44).

28. See Brock (1981).

29. See the classic work of Austin (1967) and Searle (1970).

30. This anticipates Habermas's theory of universal pragmatics in many ways. For Habermas (1979) any assertion implicitly entails four validity claims which can be made against the assertor: the claim of truth (is what is said true?); the claim of intelligibility (is what is said clear?); the claim of sincerity (does the assertor believe what she says?); the claim of rightfulness (does the assertor have the authority to make such an assertion?). For a look at the relation between Peirce's universal rhetoric and Habermas's universal pragmatics, see Liszka (1991); see also Johansen (1993: 303 ff.). For a point of contrast between Habermas and Peirce, see Misak (1994).

31. These conditions are similar to what is articulated by Karl-Otto Apel in his notion of the communication community, a concept, for which as Apel

notes, he is indebted to Peirce's concept of the community of inquirers. This particular feature of the community of inquiry is similar to Apel's symmetry condition. See Apel (1973). For a discussion of the contrast between Peirce, Apel, and Habermas on this matter, see Misak (1994).

32. This is similar, in regard to Apel's notion of the communication community, to the principle of nonexclusion. See Apel (1973).

33. The principle of noncoercion is also found in Apel's notion of the ideal communication community. See Apel (1973).

34. This idea of the public character of justification is found in Dewey's notion of the "Great Community." See Dewey (1973).

35. See chap. 2 and Michael Shapiro (1991: 23): "The triadic concept of the sign is inseparable from goal-directedness." Also see Peirce (NEM 4: 261).

36. The locus classicus of the four causes is Aristotle's *Physics*, Book II, Chapter 7.

37. See Dijksterhuis (1969).

38. See Short (1981), whose analysis of Peirce's concept of teleology I'm relying upon here. See also Potter (1967).

39. See Prigogine (1971).

40. See Short (1981: 372).

41. I'm following Short (1981) on this topic.

42. See Short (1981: 372–373).

43. See Short (1981: 373–375).

44. See Short (1981: 376); Shapiro (1991: 31).

REFERENCES

Alexander, Peter. 1965. On the Logic of Discovery. *Ratio* 7: 219–232.

Almeder, Robert. 1968. Charles Peirce and the Existence of the External World. *Transactions of the Charles S. Peirce Society* 4: 63–79.

Altschuler, Bruce. 1978. The Nature of Peirce's Pragmatism. *Transactions of the Charles S. Peirce Society* 14 (3): 147–175.

Andacht, Fernando. 1994. The Social Imaginary. Paper delivered at the Fifth Congress of the International Association of Semiotic Studies, Berkeley, California.

Andersen, Henning. 1980. Summarizing Discussion: Introduction. In *Typology and Genetics of Language*. Edited by T. Throne et al. Copenhagen: Villedsen and Christensen.

Anderson, Douglas. 1984. Peirce and Metaphor. *Transactions of the Charles S. Peirce Society* 20 (4): 453–468.

_____. 1986. The Evolution of Peirce's Concept of Abduction. *Transactions of the Charles S. Peirce Society* 22 (2).

Apel, Karl-Otto. 1973. The Communication Community and the Foundation of Ethics. *The Transformation of Philosophy*. Translated by G. Adey and D. Frisby. Boston: Routledge and Kegan Paul.

_____. 1981. *Charles S. Peirce: From Pragmatism to Pragmaticism*. Translated by J. Krois. Amherst: University of Massachusetts Press.

Austin, J. L. 1967. *How to Do Things with Words*. Cambridge: Harvard University Press.

Ayim, Maryann. 1974. Retroduction: The Rational Instinct. *Transactions of the Charles S. Peirce Society* 10: 34–43.

Barthes, Roland. 1967. *Elements of Semiology*. Translated by A. Lavers and C. Smith. New York: Hill and Wang.

Baudrillard, Jean. 1981. *For a Critique of the Political Economy of the Sign*. Translated by C. Levine. St. Louis: Telos Press.

Benedict, George. 1985. What Are Representamens? *Transactions of the Charles S. Peirce Society* 21 (2): 340–370.

Beneke, Friedrich. 1833. *Die Philosophie in ihrem Verhältnis zur Erfarhung, zur Spekulation und zum Lebe*. Berlin.

Bense, Max. 1967. *Semiotik: Allgemeine Theorie der Zeichen*. Baden-Baden: Agis.

Berry, George. 1952. Peirce's Contribution to the Logic of Statements and Quantifiers. In *Studies in the Philosophy of Charles Sanders Peirce*. Edited by P. Wiener and F. Young. Cambridge: Harvard University Press.

Bloomfield, L. 1935. *Language*. London: Holt.

Booth, Wayne. 1988. *The Company We Keep: An Ethics of Fiction*. Berkeley: University of California Press.

Braga, M. Lucia Santaella. 1988. Charles S. Peirce's Object (of the Sign). *Versus* 49: 53–58.

Braithwaite, R. B. 1934. Peirce on Probability and Induction. *Mind* 43: 500–511.

Brent, Joseph. 1993. *Charles Sanders Peirce: A Life*. Bloomington: Indiana University Press.

Brentano, Franz. 1973. *Psychology from an Empirical Standpoint*. Translated by A. Rancurello et al. New York: Humanities Press.

Brock, Jarrett. 1979. Principal Themes in Peirce's Logic of Vagueness. *Peirce Studies* 1: 41–50.

_____. 1981. An Introduction to Peirce's Theory of Speech Acts. *Transactions of the Charles S. Peirce Society* 17 (4): 319–326.

Brown, W. M. 1983. The Economy of Peirce's Abduction. *Transactions of the Charles S. Peirce Society* 19 (4): 397–412.

Burks, Arthur. 1946. Peirce's Theory of Abduction. *Philosophy of Science* 13: 301–306.

_____. 1964. Peirce's Two Theories of Probability. In *Studies in the Philosophy of Charles S. Peirce*. Edited by E. Moore and R. Robin. Amherst: University of Massachusetts Press.

Carnap, Rudolf. 1942. *Introduction to Semantics*. Cambridge: Harvard University Press.

Casteneda, Hector. 1989. The Semantics of the Causal Roles of Proper Names. *Thinking, Language and Experience*. Minneapolis: University of Minnesota Press.

Cheng, Chung-ying. 1966. Peirce's Probabilistic Theory of Inductive Validity. *Transactions of the Charles S. Peirce Society* 2: 86–112.

Clendenning, John, and Frank Oppenheim. 1990. New Documents on Josiah Royce. *Transactions of the Charles S. Peirce Society* 26 (1): 131–146.

Corrington, Robert. 1984. A Comparison of Royce's Key Notion of the Community of Interpretation with the Hermeneutics of Gadamer and Heidegger. *Transactions of the Charles S. Peirce Society* 20 (3): 279–302.

Culler, Jonathan. 1981. *The Pursuit of Signs*. Ithaca: Cornell University Press.

Deledalle, Gerard. 1967a. Peirce ou Saussure. *Semiosis* 1: 7–13.

_____. 1967b. Saussure et Peirce. *Semiosis* 2: 18–24.

Derrida, Jacques. 1978. *Of Grammatology*. Translated by G. Spivak. Baltimore: Johns Hopkins University Press.

Dewey, John. 1938. *Logic, the Theory of Inquiry*. New York: Holt.

_____. 1973. Search for the Great Community. *The Philosophy of John Dewey*. 2 vols. Edited by J. McDermott. New York: Putnam.

Dijksterhuis, E. J. 1969. *The Mechanization of the World Picture*. Oxford: Oxford University Press.

Di Paolo, J., et al. 1991. Autologous peritoneal mesothelial cell implant in rabbits and peritoneal dialysis patients. *Nephron* 57 (3): 323–331.

Dozoretz, Jerry. 1979. The Internally Real, the Fictitious, and the Indubitable. *Peirce Studies* 1: 77–88.

Fann, K. T. 1970. *Peirce's Theory of Abduction*. The Hague: Martinus Nijhoff.

Feibleman, James. 1969. *An Introduction to the Philosophy of Charles S. Peirce*. Cambridge: MIT Press.

Fisch, Max. 1978. Peirce's General Theory of Signs. In *Sight, Sound and Sense*. Edited by Thomas Sebeok. Bloomington: Indiana University Press, pp. 31–70.

————. 1986. Peirce's Arisbe: The Greek Influences in His Later Philosophy. *Peirce, Semeiotic and Pragmatism*. Bloomington: Indiana University Press.

Fisch, Max, Kenneth Ketner, and Christian Kloesel. 1979. The New Tools of Peirce Scholarship, with Particular Reference to Semiotic. *Peirce Studies* 1: 1–19.

Fisette, Jean. 1990. *Introduction à la sémiotique de C. S. Peirce*. Montreal: XYZ.

Fitzgerald, John. 1966. *Peirce's Theory of Signs as a Foundation for Pragmatism*. The Hague: Mouton.

Fries, Jakob. 1824. *System der Metaphysik*. Heidelberg.

Gadamer, Hans-Georg. 1975. *Truth and Method*. New York: Seabury Press.

Gallie, W. B. 1952. *Peirce and Pragmatism*. Harmondsworth: Penguin.

Gentry, George. 1952. Habit and the Logical Interpretant. In *Studies in the Philosophy of Charles S. Peirce*. Edited by P. Wiener and F. Young. Cambridge: Harvard University Press.

Goodman, Nelson. 1968. *Languages of Art*. New York: Bobbs-Merrill.

Goudge, Thomas. 1940. Peirce's Treatment of Induction. *Philosophy of Science* 7: 56–68.

————. 1965. Peirce's Index. *Transactions of the Charles S. Peirce Society* 1 (2): 52–70.

Greenlee, Douglas. 1973. *Peirce's Concept of Sign*. The Hague: Mouton.

Guiraud, Pierre. 1975. *Semiology*. Translated by G. Gross. London: Routledge and Kegan Paul.

Habermas, Jürgen. 1972. *Knowledge and Human Interests*. Boston: Beacon Press.

————. 1979. *Communication and the Evolution of Society*. Translated by T. McCarthy. Boston: Beacon Press.

Haley, Michael. 1988. *The Semeiosis of Poetic Metaphor*. Bloomington: Indiana University Press.

————. 1993. A Peircean "Play of Musement." In *The Peirce Seminar Papers*. Edited by M. Shapiro. Oxford: Berghahn Books.

Hardwick, Charles S. 1979. Peirce's Influence on Some British Philosophers. *Peirce Studies* 1: 25–30.

Hawkes, Terence. 1977. *Structuralism and Semiotics*. Berkeley: University of California Press.

Hawking, Stephen. 1993. *Black Holes and Baby Universes*. New York: Bantam.

Hempel, C. G. 1965. *Aspects of Scientific Explanation*. New York: Free Press.

————. 1966. *Philosophy of Natural Science*. Englewood Cliffs: Prentice-Hall.

Hilpinen, Risto. 1992. On Peirce's Philosophical Logic: Propositions and Their Objects. *Transactions of the Charles S. Peirce Society* 28 (3): 467–488.

Houser, Nathan. 1992. On Peirce's Theory of Propositions: A Response to Hilpinen. *Transactions of the Charles S. Peirce Society*. 28 (3): 489–504.

————. 1992a. Introduction. *The Essential Peirce*. Vol. 1. Edited by N. Houser and C. Kloesel. Bloomington: Indiana University Press.

Johansen, Jorgen. 1985. Prolegomena to a Semiotic Theory of Text Interpretation. *Semiotica* 57 (3/4): 225–288.

———. 1993. *Dialogic Semiosis*. Bloomington: Indiana University Press.

Johnson, Henry. 1968. The Speculative Rhetoric of Charles S. Peirce. Master's thesis, University of Florida.

Kant, Immanuel. 1956. *Critique of Practical Reason*. Translated by Lewis White Beck. Indianapolis: Bobbs-Merrill.

———. 1974. *The Critique of Judgment*. Translated by J. H. Bernard. New York: Hafner.

Kent, Beverly. 1987. *Charles S. Peirce: Logic and the Classification of Science*. Montreal: McGill–Queens University Press.

Ketner, Kenneth. 1981. The Best Example of Semiosis and Its Use in Teaching Semiotics. *American Journal of Semiotics* 1 (1/2): 47–84.

———. 1985. How Hintikka Misunderstood Peirce's Account of Theorematic Reasoning. *Transactions of the Charles S. Peirce Society* 21 (3): 407–418.

Ketner, Kenneth, and Hilary Putnam. 1992. Introduction. *Reasoning and the Logic of Things*. Edited by K. Ketner. Cambridge: Harvard University Press.

Klawans, Harold. 1991. Hollow Victory. *Discover*, December, 80–83.

Kolaga, Wojciech. 1986. *The Literary Sign: A Triadic Model*. Katowice: Uniwersytet Slaski.

Kripke, Saul. 1972. *Naming and Necessity*. Cambridge: MIT Press.

Kruse, Felicia. 1991. Genuineness and Degeneracy in Peirce's Categories. *Transactions of the Charles S. Peirce Society* 27 (3): 267–298.

Lacan, Jacques. 1957. L'instance de la lettre dans l'inconscient ou la raison depuis Freud. *La psychanalyse* 4: 47–81.

Lenz, John. 1964. Induction as Self-Corrective. In *Studies in the Philosophy of Charles S. Peirce*. Edited by E. Moore and R. Robin. Amherst: University of Massachusetts Press.

Lévi-Strauss, Claude. 1968. *The Savage Mind*. Chicago: University of Chicago Press.

Lieb, Irwin. 1953. *Charles S. Peirce's Letters to Lady Welby*. New Haven: Whitlock's.

Liszka, James Jakób. 1978. Community in C. S. Peirce: Science as a Means and as an End. *Transactions of the Charles S. Peirce Society* 14 (4): 305–321.

———. 1981. Peirce and Jakobson: Towards a Structuralist Reconstruction of Peirce. *Transactions of the Charles S. Peirce Society* 17 (1): 41–61.

———. 1989. *The Semiotic of Myth*. Bloomington: Indiana University Press.

———. 1990. Peirce's Interpretant. *Transactions of the Charles S. Peirce Society* 26 (1): 17–62.

———. 1991. Speculative Rhetoric and Universal Pragmatics. In *Proceedings of the Semiotic Society of America*. Edited by J. Deely and T. Prewitt. Washington, D.C.: University Press of America.

———. 1991a. Towards a Peircean Theory of Troping. *Cruzeiro Semiotico* 15: 111–122.

———. 1993. Peirce in France. *Semiotica* 93 (1/2): 139–153.

———. 1993a. Good and Bad Foundationalism. *Transactions of the Charles S. Peirce Society* 29 (4): 573–580.

_____. 1993b. The Valuation of the Interpretant. In *Charles S. Peirce and the Philosophy of Science*. Edited by Edward Moore. Tuscaloosa: University of Alabama Press.

_____. 1994. David Savan and the Last Signs of Peirce. In *The Peirce Seminar Papers*. Edited by M. Shapiro. Vol. 2. Oxford: Berghahn Books.

Lyne, John. 1978. Charles S. Peirce on Rhetoric and Communication. Ph.D. dissertation, University of Wisconsin.

_____. 1980. Rhetoric and Semiotic in Charles S. Peirce. *Quarterly Journal of Speech* 66: 155–168.

Martinet, Jeanne. 1980. Unpublished paper presented at the University of St. Andrews.

McKeon, Charles. 1952. Peirce's Scotistic Realism. In *Studies in the Philosophy of Charles S. Peirce*. Edited by P. Wiener and F. Young. Cambridge: Harvard University Press.

Merleau-Ponty, Maurice. 1964. *Signs*. Translated by R. McClearly. Evanston: Northwestern University Press.

Merrell, Floyd. 1990. Web, Weave or Fabric? *Semiotica* 81 (1/2): 93–133.

Merrill, G. H. 1975. Peirce on Probability and Induction. *Transactions of the Charles S. Peirce Society* 11: 90–109.

Michael, Emily. 1977. A Note on the Roots of Peirce's Division of Logic into Three Branches. *Notre Dame Journal of Formal Logic* 18: 639–640.

Mill, John Stuart. 1979. *An Examination of Sir William Hamilton's Philosophy*. In vol. 9 of *The Collected Works of John Stuart Mill*. Toronto: University of Toronto Press.

Misak, Cheryl. 1994. Pragmatism and the Transcendental Turn in Truth and Ethics. *Transactions of the Charles S. Peirce Society* 30 (4): 739–776.

Moore, Edward. 1964. The Influence of Duns Scotus on Peirce. In *Studies in the Philosophy of Charles Sanders Peirce*. Edited by E. Moore and R. Robin. Amherst: University of Massachusetts Press.

Morris, Charles. 1946. *Signs, Language and Behavior*. New York: Prentice-Hall.

Muller, Ralf. 1994. On the Principles of Construction and the Order of Peirce's Trichotomies of Signs. *Transactions of the Charles S. Peirce Society* 30 (1): 136–153.

Murphey, Murray. 1961. *The Development of Peirce's Philosophy*. Cambridge: Harvard University Press.

Niiniluoto, Ilkka. 1993. Peirce's Theory of Statistical Explanations. In *Charles S. Peirce and the Philosophy of Science*. Edited by Edward Moore. Tuscaloosa: University of Alabama Press, pp. 186–207.

Pape, Helmut. 1991. Not Every Object of a Sign Has Being. *Transactions of the Charles S. Peirce Society* 37 (2): 141–178.

_____. 1993. Final Causality in Peirce's Semiotics and His Classification of the Sciences. *Transactions of the Charles S. Peirce Society* 29 (4): 581–608.

Perreiah, Alan. 1989. Peirce's Semiotic and Scholastic Logic. *Transactions of the Charles S. Peirce Society* 25 (1): 41–49.

Peterson, John. 1983. Signs, Thirdness and Conventionalism in Peirce. *Transactions of the Charles S. Peirce Society* 19 (1): 23–28.

Potter, Vincent. 1967. *Charles S. Peirce: On Norms and Ideals.* Amherst: University of Massachusetts Press.

Prigogine, Ilya. 1971. Unity of Physical Laws and Levels of Description. In *Interpretations of Life and Mind.* Edited by M. Greene. New York.

Prower, Emmanuel. 1986. C. S. Peirce's Semiotic and the Degeneration of Signs. Dissertation, University of Silesia.

Ransdell, Joseph. 1976. Another Interpretation of Peirce's Semiotic. *Transactions of the Charles S. Peirce Society* 12 (2): 97–110.

_____. 1979. The Epistemic Function of Iconicity in Perception. *Peirce Studies* 1: 51–66.

Roberts, Don Davis. 1964. The Existential Graphs and Natural Deduction. In *Studies in the Philosophy of Charles S. Peirce.* Edited by E. Moore and R. Robin. Amherst: University of Massachusetts Press.

Rosenthal, Sandra. 1990. Peirce's Ultimate Logical Interpretant and Dynamical Object: A Pragmatic Perspective. *Transactions of the Charles S. Peirce Society* 26 (2): 195–210.

Royce, Josiah. 1968. *The Problem of Christianity.* Chicago: University of Chicago Press.

Salmon, Wesley. 1984. *Scientific Explanation and the Causal Structure of the World.* Princeton: Princeton University Press.

Sanders, Gary. 1970. Peirce's Sixty-Six Signs. *Transactions of the Charles S. Peirce Society* 6 (1): 3–16.

Saussure, Ferdinand de. 1959. *Course in General Linguistics.* Edited by C. Bally and A. Sechehaye. Translated by W. Baskin. New York: McGraw-Hill.

Savan, David. 1965. Decision and Knowledge in Peirce. *Transactions of the Charles S. Peirce Society* 1 (2): 35–51.

_____. 1977. Questions Concerning Certain Classifications Claimed for Signs. *Semiotica* 19 (3/4): 179–195.

_____. 1981. Peirce's Semiotic Theory of Emotion. In *Proceedings of the International Congress on Peirce and Semiotics.* Lubbock: Texas Tech University Press, pp. 319–333.

_____. 1981a. The Unity of Peirce's Thought. In *Pragmaticism and Purpose: Essays Presented to Thomas A. Goudge.* Edited by J. Slater, L. Summer, F. Wilson. Toronto: University of Toronto Press.

_____. 1986. Response to T. L. Short. *Transactions of the Charles S. Peirce Society* 22 (2): 125–144.

_____. 1988. *An Introduction to C. S. Peirce's Full System of Semeiotic.* Toronto: Toronto Semiotic Circle.

_____. 1988a. Peirce and the Trivium. *Cruzeiro Semiotico* 8: 50–56.

_____. 1994. C. S. Peirce and American Semiotics. In *The Peirce Seminar Papers.* Vol. 2. Edited by M. Shapiro. Oxford: Berghahn Books.

Seager, William. 1988. Peirce's Teleological Signs. *Semiotica* 69 (3/4): 303–314.

Schiller, Friedrich. 1965. *The Aesthetic Education of Man.* Translated by R. Snell. New York: Ungar.

Searle, John. 1970. *Speech Acts.* Cambridge: Cambridge University Press.

_____. 1988. *Intentionality.* Cambridge: Cambridge University Press.

Sebeok, Thomas. 1979. *The Sign and Its Masters*. Austin: University of Texas Press.

Shapiro, Michael. 1983. *The Sense of Grammar*. Bloomington: Indiana University Press.

―――. 1991. *The Sense of Change*. Bloomington: Indiana University Press.

Shapiro, Michael, and Marianne Shapiro. 1976. *Hierarchy and the Structure of Tropes*. Bloomington: Indiana University Press.

Sharpe, Robert. 1970. Induction, Abduction and the Evolution of Science. *Transactions of the Charles S. Peirce Society* 6: 17–33.

Short, Thomas. 1981. Peirce's Concept of Final Causation. *Transactions of the Charles S. Peirce Society* 17 (4): 369–383.

―――. 1981a. Semeiosis and Intentionality. *Transactions of the Charles S. Peirce Society* 27 (3): 197–223.

―――. 1982. Life among the Legisigns. *Transactions of the Charles S. Peirce Society* 18 (4): 285–310.

―――. 1984. Some Problems concerning Peirce's Conceptions of Concepts and Propositions. *Transactions of the Charles S. Peirce Society* 29 (1): 20–37.

Singer, Beth. 1983. *Ordinal Naturalism*. Bucknell: Bucknell University Press.

―――. 1987. Signs, Interpretations, and the Social World. In *Pragmatism Considers Phenomenology*. Edited by R. Corrington et al. Washington, D.C.: University Press of America, pp. 93–114.

Skagestad, Peter. 1981. *The Road to Inquiry: Charles S. Peirce's Pragmatic Realism*. New York: Columbia University Press.

Sowa, John. Forthcoming. Matching Logical Structure to Linguistic Structure. In *Studies in the Logic of Charles S. Peirce*. Bloomington: Indiana University Press.

Spiegelberg, Herbert. 1956. Husserl's and Peirce's Phenomenologies: Coincidence or Interaction. *Philosophy and Phenomenological Research* 17: 164–185.

Staat, Wim. 1993. On Abduction, Deduction, Induction and the Categories. *Transactions of the Charles S. Peirce Society* 29 (2): 225–337.

Stetter, Christian. 1979. Peirce und Saussure. *Kodikas/Code* 1: 124–149.

Thagard, Paul. 1977. The Unity of Peirce's Theory of Hypothesis. *Transactions of the Charles S. Peirce Society* 13: 112–121.

Van Fraasen, Bas. 1980. *The Scientific Image*. Oxford: Oxford University Press.

Von Wright, Georg. 1971. *Explanation and Understanding*. Ithaca: Cornell University Press.

Walther, Elisabeth. 1974. *Allgemeine Zeichenlehre: Einführung in die Grundlagen der Semiotik*. Stuttgart: Deutsche Verlags-Anstalt.

Wegener, Alfred. 1966. *The Origin of Continents and Oceans*. New York: Dover.

Weiss, Paul, and Arthur Burks. 1945. Peirce's Sixty-Six Signs. *Journal of Philosophy* 13: 382–390.

Wennerberg, Hjalmar. 1962. *The Pragmatism of C. S. Peirce*. Lund: C. W. K. Gleerup.

Zeman, J. Jay. 1986. Peirce's Philosophy of Logic. *Transactions of the Charles S. Peirce Society* 22 (1): 1–22.

INDEX

James Jakób Liszka is Professor of Philosophy at the University of Alaska Anchorage. He is the author of *The Semiotic of Myth* and several articles on semiotic and related fields. He is past editor of the *Graduate Faculty Philosophy Journal* and the *Alaska Quarterly Review*.